MYSTERIES
ON THE
HIGH SEAS

MYSTERIES
ON THE
HIGH SEAS

PHILIP MacDOUGALL

DAVID & CHARLES
Newton Abbot   London   North Pomfret (Vt)

British Library Cataloguing in Publication Data

MacDougall, Philip
  Mysteries on the high seas.
  1. Ocean
  I. Title
  001.9′4′09162   GC21

ISBN 0 7153 8422 8

Typeset by Typesetters (Birmingham) Ltd,
and printed in Great Britain
by Redwood Burn Limited, Trowbridge, Wiltshire
for David & Charles (Publishers) Limited
Brunel House Newton Abbot Devon

Published in the United States of America
by David & Charles Inc
North Pomfret Vermont 05053 USA

Contents

	List of Illustrations	7
	Introduction	9
1	Without Trace	13
2	Monsters of the Deep	25
3	The Woolwich Ship	38
4	Toll for the Brave	44
5	The Loss of the *Victoria*	56
6	The Fate of the *Waratah*	70
7	Accident or Sabotage?	81
8	A Mere Pawn	100
9	USS *Cyclops*	119
10	Fire!	129
11	Two Post-War Disappearances	136
12	Submarines	146
13	The Veronica Mutiny	157
14	Spyship?	169
15	Disaster Ships	180
	Bibliography	188
	Index	190

List of Illustrations

The fishing launch *Joyita*	17
The fishing launch *Joyita*	17
Squid attacking Captain Dens' three-masted merchantman	18
Sea monster witnessed by Hans Egede in 1734	18
King Henry VIII's *Great Galley?*	35
Carvel-built hull of Woolwich ship	36
Ribs at stern end of Woolwich ship	36
Admiral Sir George Tryon	53
Rear-Admiral Sir Albert Hastings Markham	54
Diagram showing movements of HMS *Camperdown* and HMS *Victoria*	57
The last moments of HMS *Victoria*	71
HMS *Victoria*	71
Diagram of HMS *Victoria* on the point of capsizing	72
HMS *Bulwark*	89
2 Bankside Villas, Chatham, home of John Harston	89
Memorial to those killed on HMS *Bulwark* and *Princess Irene*	89
Lusitania's lifeboats struggling to move away	90
USS *Cyclops*	107
Submarine M.1 at Venice	108
S-class submarine *Sportsman*	125
Israeli submarine *Dakar*	126
British submarine *Affray*	143
Gaul, deep-sea trawler	144
Orsino, deep-sea trawler	144

Introduction

In February 1948 the radio operator of the SS *Ourang Medan*, which he indicated to be in the Bay of Bengal close to the Adaman Sea, broadcast a garbled and strange SOS. He reported that all officers and crew were dead, whilst he himself was dying. The rescue ships which raced to the scene discovered a horrific sight. Bodies were strewn throughout the decks, with the radio operator slumped across his desk. None of the bodies revealed any sign of injury, it being impossible to determine the cause of all these deaths. A subsequent attempt to tow the vessel into the nearest port failed, the *Ourang Medan* bursting into flames. The world had been given another sea mystery . . . or had it?

The SS *Ourang Medan* was a strange ship. Although her story is included in a number of books, much of what has been written needs to be carefully scrutinised. Is it possible that the whole story is nothing more than fiction dressed up as fact? A basis of truth may exist, but the accounts given are all far too neat: a radio operator dying with his fingers still outstretched towards the transmission keys; the total lack of survivors and the vessel bursting into flames only minutes after discovery. Moreover, the report is not mentioned in any contemporary newspaper, and the *Ourang Medan* fails to be included in the usually definitive *Lloyd's Wreck Returns*. The fate of the *Ourang Medan* is not the only mystery, therefore; the very ship is a mystery!

A search for unusual maritime events produces hundreds of such stories. Those appearing in this book have been carefully verified, with any doubts about the authenticity of particular points being indicated. Where possible additional information has been given. An attempt has also been made to avoid rehashing stories that have been reprinted over and over again. For this reason the opening chapter makes only a brief reference to the

Mary Celeste, instead looking at other ships whose crews have also disappeared.

Nor should it be thought that maritime mysteries are a thing of the past: one ship is still lost every two days, and a great number still provide mystery and intrigue. Off the shores of the United Kingdom alone, there have recently been several unexplained events. In December 1981, for instance, the *Mark*, a Panamanian-registered freighter of 499 tons, simply disappeared in a violent storm. Seven months later, in July 1982, the Breton trawler *Galu Ar Mor* sank in the Irish Channel, possibly dragged backwards by a submarine caught in her nets. In September of the same year, the 500 ton Irish-registered coaster *Majorca* sank off the Devon coast for no apparent reason. The seas at the time were described as exceptionally calm, and the Brixham coastguard was not prepared to accept the suggested possibility of her cargo having shifted. Finally, throughout 1982, a diving team was involved in helping to solve one earlier mystery: the sinking of the *Lusitania*. According to German accounts she was sunk during May 1915 because she was being used to carry ammunition, a point denied by the Admiralty. The evidence of the diving team, although not conclusive, seems to favour the German version.

The following chapters are a selection of mysteries drawn from around the world. If there is a slight bias to British ships, this must be excused. After all, ships of this nationality once dominated the world, with the red and white ensigns only now becoming a less frequent sight. Additionally, of course, based in Britain, it is easier to research those particular vessels. Naturally I hope this does not detract from the book in any way. In writing it, though, I greatly enjoyed giving thought to a host of insoluble problems. Which, if any, of the suggested causes happened to those numerous ships whose histories are recorded on the following pages? For the most part, nothing more will ever be known.

Finally, I would like to give thanks to all those who assisted in the writing of this book. In particular, I would like to mention Mr

R. A. Beattie, Miss Pat O'Driscoll, Mr Peter Marsden, Mr Dave Sellers and Mr Willie Wadlow. Also Gus Britton of the Royal Navy Submarine Museum, Mr Mike Maddison of Thames Television and Ms Lucia W. Woodland of the *Virginia Pilot.* Additionally, I would like to thank the staff of the following libraries and institutions: British Museum Newspaper Library, Cornwall County Library, Gillingham Public Library, Greater London Council Photographic Library, Lewisham Public Libraries, Lloyd's Shipping Information Services, Royal Institution of Naval Architects' library, Scheepvaartmuseum in Holland, together with the International Maritime Organisation and the French and Israeli embassies.

Philip MacDougall

1
Without Trace

One single vessel, the *Mary Celeste*, can undoubtedly be considered the very epitome of all maritime mysteries. Abandoned in mid-Atlantic during the winter of 1872, she has continued to puzzle the world ever since. Why should the crew of a perfectly sound ship simply take to the rowing boat, never to be seen again? Whilst little need be said about the *Mary Celeste*, far too much is to be found elsewhere; a few words are in order if only to set the scene.

It was the British barque *Dei Gratia* that first discovered the drifting derelict, recognising her to be in some sort of trouble as the only sails set were on the foremast and jib. Three crew members eventually boarded the *Mary Celeste*, assisting her later entry into Gibraltar Harbour. Doubtless the entire crew of the *Dei Gratia* thought it all worthwhile, each receiving a share of the £1,700 salvage value. At the time, many of those living in Gibraltar clearly considered the whole affair as part of an involved attempt at fraud. Those who supported this theory pointed to the fact that both ships had recently left New York, and that the two captains were probably acquainted. Indeed, as far as this last point was concerned, it was later discovered that both captains had actually dined together on the night prior to the departure of the *Mary Celeste* − a fact then unknown in Gibraltar.

Thoughts of the *Mary Celeste* were revived somewhat more recently. In October 1955 crew and passengers on the 70 ton fishing launch *Joyita* disappeared in circumstances equally as mysterious. Leaving Apia, the capital of Western Samoa, on Sunday 5 October, she was bound for the Tokelau Islands, a New Zealand mandate some 700 miles to the north. On board the

13

small craft were twenty-five people, sixteen crew members and nine passengers – most of the latter officials of the New Zealand government.

At the time, the *Joyita* had been chartered for Roger Peerless, newly appointed district officer to the Tokelau Islands. An enthusiastic twenty-nine-year-old, he wished to visit his newly won charge at the earliest available opportunity. As the *Joyita* was a fairly sizeable craft, it was also agreed to take quantities of food to the islands, together with a group of returning natives. One other passenger should also be mentioned, George Williams, an employee of E. A. Coxon & Co Ltd, an island trading concern. Carrying £1,000 in cash, he was empowered to purchase some of the islands' copra yield for loading on to the *Joyita*.

Master-in-charge of the launch was T. H. Miller, known as 'Dusty' to his friends. Originally born in Cardiff, he had become an officer in the Naval Reserve, spending much of his war service in the Pacific. Presumably he had grown attached to this area of the world, for he had remained there ever since. Not one of the world's most successful characters, he had acquired the *Joyita* for his own personal use, mostly engaging in tuna fishing. Rarely, however, did he have sufficient money to keep the launch in repair. Indeed, during the five months prior to the *Joyita* leaving Apia she had remained totally idle, Dusty Miller having insufficient funds to keep her at sea.

As for the *Joyita* herself, she had been built back in 1931. A typical rich man's fishing launch, she had swivel chairs, a deep freeze section, luxurious accommodation and, perhaps most useful of all, a high-powered radio. American registered, she had been commandeered during the war, and used by the navy as a patrol vessel. She was 69ft long with a 7ft 6in draught and had two 225hp diesel engines. Moreover, at a later period the vessel had been fully insulated with cork, making her unsinkable.

The voyage to the Tokelau Islands should have taken no more than two days – but it was soon clear that something might well have gone wrong. Within a few hours of sailing, Miller had failed to make his first radio check. This was sufficient to alert the authorities, and a Royal New Zealand Air Force Sunderland was soon combing the approximate course taken by the fishing launch. At first, of course, nobody really felt that the crew and passengers were endangered, both visibility and weather conditions being particularly good. When, however, the *Joyita* failed to arrive at Fakaofu, her port of destination, the air and sea search was immediately stepped up. Over the next few weeks seaplanes were to comb thoroughly a 100,000 square-mile zone, but nothing was to be seen of the launch.

It was not until 10 November, a full five weeks after the *Joyita*'s departure from Apia, that anything further was heard of the vessel. On that day, the surprised crew of the Fijian steamer *Tuvalu* found the *Joyita* drifting in a waterlogged condition. Almost a thousand miles from her original course, being 90 miles north of Vanua Levu, one of the islands in the Fijian group, she had been completely abandoned. Closer inspection revealed that many of her compartments were flooded, whilst the port side of her superstructure was missing: blown or washed away. It was also noted that a canvas awning had been rigged on deck, apparently following whatever had befallen her, and had been used as a shelter from the sun. With the discovery quickly reported to the harbour-master at Suva, the nearest large port, thoughts turned to the *Mary Celeste*. In a statement, subsequently reported in virtually every newspaper in the world, Suva's harbour-master simply declared the launch to be another *Mary Celeste*, with no logical explanation for the disappearance of those on board.

Throughout the following months, the Fiji Islands were besieged by newspaper and television reporters. Whereas the original *Mary Celeste* had been more or less ignored back in 1872, this twentieth-century mystery was to be given a very different treatment. Every theory, however unlikely, was to be given massive worldwide coverage. Tidal waves, waterspouts and pirates were all claimed as possible solutions. One idea followed another, each being discarded in the quest for something even more sensational. Most dramatic of all, perhaps, was the view originally offered by the 19 November edition of the *Fiji Times and Herald*. In a banner headline it was loudly proclaimed that 'All Aboard the Joyita Murdered'. Declaring this to be the official view of the Fijian administration, the lead article went on to state that each and every person on board the *Joyita* had been killed by members of a Japanese fishing fleet:

> . . . it is assumed that the Joyita innocently ran through the Japanese fleet and that the Joyita's people saw something the Japanese did not want them to see. There was a young District Officer on board (Mr Peerless) who possibly protested at what he saw.
>
> The suggestion is that resentful Japanese boarded the Joyita, murdered or took prisoner the passengers and crew . . .

As evidence, reference was made to an open seacock, said to have resulted from an attempt to scuttle the launch, together with indications of a fire said to have broken out. Further:

> A steering chain on one side of the Joyita was broken and this is thought to have been done by the Japanese as well.

Within hours, however, the story was being denied. In a statement broadcast throughout the islands, A. F. R. Stoddart, the colonial secretary, declared:

> . . . such examination of her contents as has so far been possible supports the suggestion that the cause of the disaster was natural causes – that is to say, that she was overwhelmed as a result of some freak of weather at a time when perhaps her engines were stopped.

With the *Joyita* having been towed into port, she arrived at Suva on 13 November, and a full investigation was soon undertaken. At that time it was discovered that the log was missing and that there was no sign of the £1,000 carried by George Williams. No damage to the hull was detected, so ruling out collision, whilst everything moveable had been stripped. Earlier reports of a fire were also shown to be incorrect, the examination revealing that such charred areas were at least one year old and that the damage to saloon timbers had been covered with panelling, since torn away.

As examination of the launch continued, the mystery only

A modern *Mary Celeste*. On 10 November 1955 the 70 ton fishing launch *Joyita* was found abandoned north of the Fijian islands. Nothing has ever been discovered of her nine passengers and sixteen crew, nor why the vessel should have been abandoned in the first place. That she was in a waterlogged condition is obvious, but damage to the craft was relatively minor, and she could easily have supported all on board *(Ministry of Information, Fiji)*

What strange unusual creatures lie in the depths of the ocean? At the end of the eighteenth century this three-masted merchantman, captained by Jean Magnus Dens, was attacked by a 60ft squid. At the time few believed that such an incident could ever have taken place, but the giant squid is now an accepted fact of life

The sea monster witnessed by Hans Egede in July 1734

deepened. There seemed no logical explanation for her abandonment. Even in the waterlogged condition in which she had been discovered, the *Joyita* was still able to support twenty-five individuals. Much of the damage was consistent with forty-one days of continual rocking at sea, and amongst the crew were several natives of the Gilbert Islands, considered to be some of the best seamen in the world. Food was also plentiful, some having been carried as cargo, whilst additional fishing lines would have allowed a certain variety of diet.

A final report on the *Joyita*, this time issued by the New Zealand government, still did not solve the mystery. It was declared that the launch was victim of mechanical failure. According to this report, the *Joyita* was brought to a standstill when a 1in galvanised pipe, forming part of the cooling system, had sheared; this had also led to a partial flooding of the launch. A contributory factor was the failure of the oil-pipe bilge pumps, probably through a rubbish blockage caused by the absence of strainers. However, the enquiry completely failed to explain why those on board should have left the vessel. Indeed, the enquiry declared itself completely mystified on this particular point. In the words of the report:

> Although a theory was put forward by one of the expert witnesses that many members of the crew and passengers were washed overboard at once when a wave swept away the port side of the superstructure, your Commissioners find themselves unable to subscribe with any confidence to this explanation. Though some of the ship's personnel may have been washed overboard and lost, it is, from the viewpoint of your Commissioners, very unlikely that all persons on board, including the master, should have been huddled together in that one spot and that the force of a wave was so great that all persons were immediately washed overboard in such a way that none of them, even the Gilbertese and Tokelau Islanders, who are almost as much at home in the water as they are on dry land, was able to regain the ship.

A particularly intriguing theory as to the fate of both crew and passengers of the *Joyita* was later put forward by Robin Maughan in a book entitled *The Joyita Mystery*. Interviewing a number of people who had either known Dusty Miller or had witnessed the

Joyita upon her arrival at Suva, he uncovered a number of points missed by the enquiry. Maughan started with the frequently verified fact that Miller, knowing the *Joyita* to be unsinkable, would never have abandoned the vessel. This, and the discovery of a bloodstained bandage, needle and gut, something not revealed at the enquiry, led Maughan to speculate that a fight had occurred on board, with Miller the injured party. Suggesting that this had occurred after the engine had ceased functioning, Maughan went on to propose that passengers and crew, on sighting a small island, and mistakenly afraid that the launch was about to sink, had desperately taken to the Carley floats, believing they would be able to steer towards dry land. Miller, still unconscious, was unable to advise against such a move. Later, in attempting to explain the disappearance of all movable objects, including the large cash sum, Maughan suggests the *Joyita* was boarded and plundered by the crew of an unknown fishing boat.

Another twentieth-century vessel to divest herself of a crew was the *Zebrina*, a schooner involved in the cross-Channel coal trade. It was early on the morning of 17 October 1917 that she ran aground on Rozel Point, near Dielette, France. In good order, she was, nevertheless, completely crewless. Apparently, whilst sailing between Falmouth and the Breton port of St Brieuc, something peculiar, had happened. Her boat was still in position and there were no signs of bloodshed or external damage.

It had been on 15 October that the *Zebrina* had set out from the busy West Country port of Falmouth. The war, of course, was at its height, and there were constant fears of submarine attacks. For the *Zebrina* these fears were accentuated by her inability to join an escorted convoy. An old sailing vessel, her dependence upon the wind gave her an unpredictability that was best allowed for by a separate passage. Registered in Faversham and built in 1876 by the Whitstable Shipping Co, she had a length of just on 109ft and a beam of 24½ft. Barquentine rigged — that is fore-and-aft sails on the mizzen mast and square sails on the foremast — she was extremely economical of manpower, requiring a crew of no more than five.

The *Zebrina* had actually been at Falmouth since the beginning of the month. Her cargo had been loaded at Swansea, but bad weather had since prevented her from sailing. However, safely moored though she was, she was also losing money. As such, she could not ride out the storm for ever. Indeed, she had made one fruitless effort at departure already. On 12 October, following a drop in wind, she had left Falmouth, hoping to make the French coast sometime on the next day. Her efforts, however, were thwarted. Within hours, treacherous westerly gales forced her return.

On Sunday 15 October, the *Zebrina* once again made her departure. Winds had now fallen to 11 knots, somewhat more suited to a three-masted schooner. Further, being south-westerlies, they were set fair for the coast of France. As they departed Falmouth the crew expected a smooth journey and a quick return – none could have imagined this as their last voyage.

Upon her discovery, run aground off Rozel, the Admiralty immediately assumed her to be a wartime casualty. The reason for this is a little obscure. Possibly they felt she had been attacked by a submarine and the crew removed prior to torpedoing. That she was not sunk, so the reasoning must have gone, was due to the submarine being discovered and having crash-dived. Further, the submarine must itself have been destroyed, taking the crew of the *Zebrina* to their grave. Much of this, though, does not really add up. German submarines, by this stage of the war, were not in the habit of removing crews, whilst the Admiralty had had no reports of a U-boat being sighted near a sailing vessel such as the *Zebrina*.

Perhaps, though, the *Zebrina* mystery was solved at a later point in time. In his *When Ships Go Down*, David Masters records how he carefully set out to discover exactly what did happen to the crew. Uncovering some of the evidence, he also viewed weather conditions on 16 October. From this it appears that the earlier storms once again returned. As such, no submarine could have operated on this day. He concludes, therefore, that the crew of the *Zebrina* were washed overboard:

> Think of the heavily laden schooner labouring in these seas, the waves crashing down on her and sweeping her from time to time, waves from five times to eight times her own freeboard! If she were not a good ship she would not have survived all these years, and although we can imagine her riding most of the seas, now and again a devilish monster would crash down on her with a smashing force.

As to what happened to the *Zebrina* after she had lost her crew, Masters continues:

> It is interesting to trace what would happen when the full force of the gale struck the ship and washed the crew overboard on the evening of the 16th. Left to herself, she would at once come up into the wind, and drift and be blown backward along the course followed by the gale. If the tide be taken into account and the line of depression traced on the chart we might expect her to come ashore more or less in the position she was found.

Having considered the *Joyita* and *Zebrina*, together with a brief reference to the *Mary Celeste*, it might be of interest to consider the *Harmanna* a Dutch vessel which, as far as British maritime writers are concerned, has remained a mystery since the crew departed her in March 1849. Discovered 10 miles south-east of the Eddystone Lighthouse, she was the obvious victim of a major collision. Her starboard side was heavily damaged and her bulwark had been carried away. Obviously brought to a sudden halt, she had also been dismasted. That a collision had occurred was amply demonstrated by the other vessel having left, wedged into the roundhouse, part of her figurehead and bows.

At the time it was surmised that the crew of the *Harmanna*, fearing that their vessel was about to sink, had abandoned her. That her single lifeboat was in place led to the further assumption that the crew had joined the other vessel, believing her to be less damaged. As far as contemporary English newspapers were concerned, nothing more was heard of the missing crew. Elliott O'Donnell, writing in 1926, suggested they had, in fact, joined a vessel more seriously damaged than originally suspected, its sinking at some point in the Channel or Atlantic accounting for the mystery.

Yet all this is based on limited research. Elliott O'Donnell should really have referred to newspapers of the *Harmanna*'s home town area of Wischoten. There he would have solved a mystery which he himself was helping to create. The *Groninger Courant* contains three references to the incident, stretching over a period of six weeks. The first, dated 10 April 1849, merely announces her discovery as a derelict, and the fact that she was towed into Sutton Pool by a local fishing vessel. It is also recorded that her captain and owner, Derk H. Houwink, probably had his wife and young child on board at the time.

The *Groninger Courant* of 13 April carries a longer description, concentrating on the evidence of the collision. It is stated that the other ship, at that time still unidentified, left behind part of her own gilded figurehead together with 8ft of oaken timber hull. This was sufficient for the newspaper to suggest that the *Harmanna* had been rammed by an American boat of approximately 250–300 tons.

Finally, in the edition of 22 May the mystery is solved. Details of a letter are published in which Captain Houwink, then in New York, states that during the night of 30 March, the *Harmanna* had been run down by the Le Havre to New York packet. Damage to his own ship was thought to have been extensive, much of the rigging going overboard. It was also presumed that the bottom was also damaged and that it might be better to examine the ship in the morning. Unfortunately for Captain Houwink, the *Harmanna* seems to have drifted during the night, no signs being visible at sunrise. Passengers on board the packet, concerned at the delay, prevailed upon their own captain to continue on to America. With no possibility of being landed, the entire crew of the *Harmanna*, together with the Houwink family, were taken on to New York.

Would it that all disappearing-crew mysteries could be solved so easily. Unlike the *Harmanna*, however, the various other ships mentioned showed remarkably fewer signs of damage prior to being abandoned. Perhaps, as is suggested for the *Zebrina*, they were washed overboard, but this is no more than speculation.

Alternatively, when reconsidering the *Mary Celeste*, fraud could well have been involved, but surely someone, within a decade or two of the event, would have spoken out. As for the *Joyita*, she virtually defies all explanation. Even that put forward by Robin Maughan must be questioned, relying as it does upon the existence of pirates, the proximity of an island at one particular vital moment and a fight on board. Whatever the case, therefore, the *Zebrina*, but more particularly the *Mary Celeste* and *Joyita*, will remain permanent mysteries of the sea.

2
Monsters of the Deep

With its very existence at one time doubted, the giant squid is one of the many strange and incredible creatures that are to be found in the depths of the ocean. Dangerous in the extreme, having eight huge arms and two very long tentacles, each covered with rows of suckers, they are prepared to attack anything that might be considered food. Positive proof of their existence first emerged during the nineteenth century, resulting from a number of sightings along the Newfoundland coastline. In 1871, for instance, a 15ft squid, small by later standards, was washed up on those shores. Two years later, in October 1873, a much larger squid was reported, this time said to be of 60ft. Attacking a small vessel sailing off St John's, the crew managed to save themselves when they hacked one of the creature's arms.

Following the fishing-boat incident, reports of squids in this area became so frequent that scientists came grudgingly to accept that a foundation of truth existed. Most impressive, and certainly beyond denial, was a particularly monstrous beast, this time fully confirmed as being 60ft in length, washed ashore at Thimble Thicket, Newfoundland, in November 1878. At about this time, reports of squids were also received from such diverse areas as Japan and Norway.

Given their size, and since proven voracity, the giant squid is obviously a potential danger to those who travel the seas, especially if their vessels are frail. This point, if newspaper accounts are to be believed, was demonstrated in 1874 when the British schooner *Pearl* was attacked by just such a monster. At the time, the schooner was trading in the mysterious waters of the Indian Ocean, it being the era of Krakatoa's activity. This huge volcano, eventually to erupt in 1883, had already been responsible for a number of underwater explosions, disturbing the normally placid depths.

Sometime around 7 May, the *Pearl* could have been seen leaving the port of Galle, a busy township on what is now the west coast of Sri Lanka. Having called in for water, she was merely resuming her passage to Rangoon where she was expected to take on a cargo of padding. On 10 May, having made very little seaway, she found herself completely becalmed in the Bay of Bengal. Fortunately, an evening breeze could be expected, and crew members waited patiently for the sails to swell.

Each member of the crew occupied himself in one of several ways. Some slept, others exchanged yarns, whilst the master peered expectantly to port. At first he engaged himself in observing the lines of a steamer, no more than two miles away. On this hot, sultry day, James Floyd, captain of the 150 ton *Pearl* doubtless envied all those on board the *Strathowen*, for this was the name of the cargo ship whose recently fitted boilers made her quite oblivious to the tranquil conditions that waylaid the schooner.

Elsewhere on board the *Pearl* was the mate, Bill Darling. A native of Newfoundland, he had a wealth of seagoing experience. Amongst the tales he could recount were of the times when fellow Newfoundlanders had come upon the dead remains of the fabled kraken, or giant squid. Of course, few on board believed him, it was all too fanciful; the kraken was a creature of Norse mythology, it just could not exist. Yet all on board were quickly to change their views; the *Pearl* was about to become victim to one such giant creature.

It was the captain, still engaged in viewing the *Strathowen*, who first noticed the strange object located but half a mile away. Appearing somewhat like the back of a whale, it sloped considerably less and was of a brownish colour. None of those on deck could even guess what it might be and James Floyd, wishing to break the monotony of a long sea voyage, slipped below for his rifle.

At this point Bill Darling returned to the upper deck, interested to discover what the sudden commotion was about. At once he recognised the object for what it was – a giant squid. He also knew of its dangers: 'Have a care, master, that 'ere's a squid, and will capsize us if we hurt him.' Floyd chose to ignore what subsequently turned out to be very sound advice. A crack of a rifle resounded, and the beast gave a shudder; the schooner was now doomed.

The bullet having created no more than an irritation, merely served to draw the creature's attention to the stranded vessel. Turning towards the schooner, it clearly showed that its intention was that of attack. The mate, more experienced in such matters, took charge: 'Out with your axes and knives and cut any part of him that comes aboard; look alive and Lord help us!'

As it approached, the crew more clearly saw their dangerous adversary. It was later described by the master as an oblong mass that moved by jerks. The body alone he reckoned to be more than twice the size of the schooner, whilst the arms and tentacles spread out another 100ft. By any terms it was massive. Within seconds the vessel was struck, quivering from stem to stern. Simultaneously, huge monstrous arms, each the size of a tree, seized parts of the vessel, pulling her to one side. Most of the crew were too terrified to move. Even the master, whose stupidity had caused the onslaught, was transfixed. Only a loud shout from the mate pulled them out of their combined stupor: 'Slash for your lives!'

Try as they might, however, none of the crew managed to inflict sufficient injury, and the creature maintained its grip. As might be expected, the vessel itself began to tilt dangerously, with shifting ballast creating an ever more treacherous situation. Soon the crew had little alternative. With the order given, they abandoned ship, some managing to swim towards the *Strathowen*. Most, indeed were to escape, although one of the hands found himself trapped between the main mast and a huge cephalopodic arm. Perhaps he was crushed, drowned or eaten alive. None of the surviving crew members witnessed his eventual end.

On board the *Strathowen* most of these events were witnessed by an amazed crew. The captain of the steamer, for one, had been observing the schooner through a pair of binoculars, noticing the strange object which he first considered to be a bank of seaweed. As he watched, this great mass, hitherto motionless, moved towards the *Pearl*. As it struck, the schooner visibly reeled, then righted itself. A short interlude appeared to be followed by the swaying of the masts, with the enormous mass appearing to coalesce with the rapidly sinking schooner. Eventually the crew of the *Strathowen* were to witness the *Pearl* brought on to her beam ends, lying there for a few seconds, and then disappearing into the depths below. A cry of horror arose, and the *Strathowen* made for the survivors.

Although, as mentioned, science now accepts the existence of giant squids, none matching the sheer size of that which sank the *Pearl* has yet been verified. However, one similar incident, this time involving a squid of 60ft, a much more acceptable size, was apparently told to the French naturalist Denys de Montfort. It appears that at about the turn of the eighteenth century a certain Danish vessel, captained by one Jean Magnus Dens, narrowly avoided destruction whilst off the coast of West Africa. Again, the vessel was becalmed and in order to utilise otherwise wasted time, Captain Dens had members of the crew cleaning and scraping much of the upper hull. Three of his men were apparently at work, standing upon planks slung over the side, when a large creature rose from the water and threw a giant tentacle around two of the sailors, pulling them underwater. In an attempt to rescue the two men, several harpoons were driven into the monster, but to no avail.

If, as is now obviously the case, the giant squid exists, perhaps there is also room in the oceans for that other mysterious beast – the sea serpent. A further monster of the depths, its existence is based entirely upon numerous sightings that are as old as written history. Indeed, one writer, Dr Bernard Heuvelmans, has gone so far as to classify several types of serpents of which he suggests the 'long-necked' variety to be the most common. According to numerous witnesses this is some 60ft in length, has a small seal-like head and a rather bulky body. Most reports of this particular creature have been in warmer regions. Another regularly witnessed serpent, the 'merhorse', has an elongated body with a mane hanging down its long neck. Amongst other serpents accorded names by Dr Heuvelmans are the 'many humped' and the 'marine saurian', the latter having the general appearance of a massive crocodile.

Earliest reports of the sea serpent have to be regarded with considerable scepticism mixed, as they are, with ancient beliefs and fables. Accounts start to become a little more believable during the eighteenth century with Hans Egede, a Scandinavian priest, giving us this account of a sea monster that showed itself during a missionary voyage to Greenland:

> On the 6th of July, 1734, when off the south coast of Greenland, a sea monster appeared to us, whose head, when raised, was on a level with our main top. Its snout was long and sharp, and it blew water almost like a whale; it had large broad paws; its body was covered with scales; its skin was rough and uneven; in other respects it was as a serpent; and when it dived, its tail, which was raised in the air, appeared to be a whole ship's length from its body.

Dr Heuvelmans has likened this particular serpent to a type he calls the 'super otter'. Amongst its chief characteristics are those of an extremely long body, shaped much like that of an otter, together with an elongated head that tapers towards the snout and two pairs of webbed feet. Dr Heuvelmans also considers that, from later sightings, it has the ability to swim like an otter by means of undulating an extremely flexible body. Restricted to northern waters, most sightings seem to have occurred along the Scandinavian coastline. In 1746, Captain Lorenz von Ferry, a Norwegian naval captain, whilst voyaging between Trondheim and Molde also sighted the 'super otter', subsequently writing this account:

> The head of this snake, which it held more than two feet above the surface of the water, resembled that of a horse. It was of a greyish colour and the mouth was quite black, and very large. It had large

29

black eyes, and a long white mane, that hung down to the surface of the water. Besides the head and the neck, we saw seven or eight folds, or coils of this snake, which were very thick, and as far as we could guess there was a fathom's distance between each fold.

On the other side of the Atlantic, the American coastline seems to have attracted the 'many humped'. During the early part of the nineteenth century a number of sightings occurred along the New England coastline, these virtually becoming a daily occurrence. For a time, the serpent seems to have taken up residence in Gloucester Harbour, with masses of people specially travelling to the area so that they might glimpse the monster. Rarely were they disappointed. Typical was this sworn account given by Matthew Gaffney, a ship's carpenter, who saw the serpent on 14 August 1817:

I was in a boat, and was within forty feet of him. His head appeared full as large as a four gallon keg, his body as large as a barrel, and his length that I saw I should judge forty feet, at least. The top of his head was of a dark colour, and the under part of his head apparently nearly white, as did also several feet of his belly that I saw.

Matthew Gaffney also claimed to have seen the serpent on numerous other occasions, but never as clearly as on that day.

Another sighting in Gloucester Harbour, taking place only two days later, was recalled by Col T. H. Perkins, who at the time was seated on a piece of land that protruded right into the harbour. Perceiving something like a huge snake, the colonel gave a loud exclamation:

A few minutes later I saw on the opposite side of the harbour, at about two miles' distance from where I had first seen, or thought I saw, the snake, the same object moving with a rapid motion up the harbour on the western shore. As it approached us, it was easy to see that its motion was not that of the common snake, either on the land or in the water, but evidently the vertical movement of the caterpillar. As nearly as I could judge, there was visible at a time about 40ft of its body. It was not, to be sure, a continuity of body, as the form from head to tail (except, as the apparent bunches appeared, as it moved through the water), was seen only at 3 or 4ft asunder. It was very evident, however, that its length must have been greater than what it appeared, as, in its movement, it left a considerable wake in its rear. I had a fine glass, and was within one-third to half a mile of it.

From the various accounts, many of them collected by a local scientific society, the frequently sighted serpent was probably about 65ft in length and about 1ft wide. Its head, which was frequently described as being flattened, was usually held some 2—3ft out of the water. Of its humps, these were certainly mentioned by a majority of witnesses, all agreeing that the number varied between ten and twenty. The serpent appeared particularly at home in the water, being able to swim at speeds in excess of 20 knots, whilst it had incredible diving abilities. At no time was it reported to show any signs of aggression, taking little notice of small boats. Sightings of the monster continued to be made for a good many years, with one of the last occurring in 1877.

It was in 1848 that the sea-serpent debate finally launched itself upon the British populace. A nation much noted for its scepticism, the numerous 'foreign' sightings had been treated with something approaching contempt. Few thought them to be anything more than fanciful dreams, condemning many of the witnesses as participants in a hoax to achieve personal fame. In October of that year, however, Captain Peter M'Quhae, commander of the Royal Navy sloop *Daedalus*, filed a detailed report to the Admiralty in which he described the sighting of 'an enormous serpent' whilst on passage from the East Indies. Of the 'long-necked' variety, it was described as having 'head and shoulders kept about four feet constantly above the surface of the sea, and nearly as we could approximate by comparing it with the length of what our main-topsail yard would show in the water, there was at least 60 feet of the animal'. Remaining on a parallel course with the vessel for about twenty minutes, it swam at a speed of about 12—15 knots, apparently on some determined purpose. M'Quhae went on to state:

It had no fins, but something like the mane of a horse, or rather a bunch of seaweed, washed about its back.

31

Another interesting sighting, this time in the Gulf of Aden, was made during the year 1879. In January of that year various individuals on board the *City of Baltimore*, on passage from India, sighted what was probably a 'long-necked' sea serpent. Amongst the witnesses was Major Senior, a member of the Bengal Staff Corps, returning to England. His description of the serpent was to appear in the *Graphic*:

> The head and neck, about two feet in diameter, rose out of the water to a height of about twenty or thirty feet, and the monster opened its jaw wide as it rose, and closed them again as it lowered its head and darted forward for a dive, reappearing almost immediately some hundred yards ahead. The body was not visible at all, and must have been some depth under water, as the disturbance on the water was too slight to attract notice, although occasionally a splash was seen at some distance behind the head. The shape of the head was not unlike pictures of the dragon I have often seen, with a bull-dog appearance of the fore-head and eyebrow. When the monster had drawn its head sufficiently out of the water, it let itself drop, as it were, like a huge log of wood, prior to darting forward under the water.

Throughout the nineteenth century there continued to be a great number of sea-serpent sightings, with about two a year usually being reported. Undoubtedly there were also a great number of unreported sightings, as one had to be very brave in order to withstand the instant ridicule that such an announcement would bring. Captain Cringle of the steamer *Umfuli* was one such unwitting victim. In December 1893 he reported a 'long-necked' serpent which he had seen off Cape Blanc, Mauritania. In a sober and highly convincing account, he told of how the creature, which was visible for over an hour, rushed at great speed 'throwing water from its breast as a vessel throws water from its bows'. Soon, though, the captain was taken to task, becoming victim to a group of narrow-minded individuals. As the captain himself later declared:

> I have been so ridiculed about the thing that I have many times wished that anybody else had seen that sea monster rather than me. I have been told that it was a string of porpoises, that it was an island of seaweed, and I do not know what besides. But if an island of seaweed

can travel at the rate of fourteen knots, or if a string of porpoises can stand 15ft out of the water, then I give in, and confess myself deceived. Such, however, could not be.

The twentieth century was also to bring numerous sightings. Amongst these were reports of the sea saurian, the serpent that resembles a large crocodile. On 30 July 1915, with World War I at its height, the German submarine U-28, then operating in the North Atlantic, successfully sank the British steamer *Iberian*. The captain of the U-boat, George Gunther Freiherr von Forstner, reported that 30 seconds after the British cargo boat disappeared below the surface there was a violent explosion which threw to the surface a large amount of wreckage. It appears that the force of the explosion, presumably occurring in one of the boilers, pushed a gigantic sea animal to the surface, the creature writhing and struggling wildly. As the U-boat was surfaced at the time, an additional four members of the crew, all on the conning tower, saw the animal which was thrown to a height of 60–100ft. According to von Forstner, it was about 60ft long, like a crocodile in shape, had four limbs with powerful webbed feet and a long tail tapering towards a point. Later in the war, in July 1918, the crew of a second U-boat, the U-109, reported seeing a sea saurian, this time in the North Sea. With an estimated length of 100ft it was described as having 'a long head, jaws like a crocodiles and legs with very definite feet'.

As to the 'merhorse', a great number of sightings seem to have occurred along the coastline of British Columbia. During the 1930s it was to appear so frequently that the beast was even given a pet name, being christened 'Caddy' – it having once been sighted at Cadboro, Victoria. Numerous of those who claimed to have seen the animal were highly respected local citizens, most of whom agreed that the beast was of an enormous length – possibly 80ft or more – and had a distinct mane that appeared to be not unlike seaweed. One went so far as to suggest that it was an animal of an earlier age, its presence changing the whole landscape. 'Caddy', it appears, was not just a twentieth-century phenomenon, investigators uncovering the fact that local

33

Chinook Indians also knew of its presence, bestowing upon it the name 'Hiachuckaluck'.

Another serpent with a similarly long history would appear to be the 'Kilindini Monster' of Mombasa. Local inhabitants had certainly known of its existence for a great number of years, but it was not until 1948 that reports began to reach European and American newspapers. Towards the end of that year, two RAF corporals apparently sighted the creature, describing it as having a large flat grey head covered with scales. Early in the following year, further reports indicated it to have been seen by a number of seamen and residents of Likoni. Such sightings doubtless continued into the 'fifties, but failed to be reported in the international press.

The British coastline, too, has generated a large number of sightings, these occurrings in such diverse areas as the Firth of Clyde (1953), Skegness (1966) and Helensburgh (1962). Most frequent of all, however, are those that take place in the West Country. In 1975, for instance, a huge creature closely resembling the 'long-necked' was seen off Pendennis Point, with sightings near Falmouth during the following year. In fact, so frequently has it been seen that like a number of other sea serpents, it has been given an affectionate name – locals calling it 'Morgawr', meaning sea giant.

This, of course, is not the end of the sea-serpent story. Sightings, for one thing, will doubtless continue. Maybe the mystery will never be cleared up, but this seems unlikely. Underneath the oceans there are some very strange creatures and one day their existence is likely to be fully confirmed. But it will be no easy task. Already fewer sightings occur at sea, these animals preferring to avoid modern ships and their noisy engines.

King Henry VIII's *Great Galley?* In November 1912, while excavation work for a new power station was underway, labourers at Woolwich uncovered the remains of a large Tudor warship. Evidence points to her being one of three vessels, of which one possibility is the *Great Galley*, launched in 1515 (*Greater London Council Photograph Library*)

Considered unimportant at the time, the Woolwich ship was allowed to decay, with no effort at preservation. This was most unfortunate as her method of construction, similar to that of the *Mary Rose*, show her to be an early example of a carvel-built warship *(Greater London Council Photograph Library)*

A further view of the Woolwich ship, this time showing her ribs at the stern end. Gaps between the planking were caulked, and then sealed with strips of timber *(Greater London Council Photograph Library)*

For this reason, it was John Ridgeway, whilst with Chay Blyth during their epic rowing feat, who was fortunate enough to make one of the last seagoing sightings. At the time their boat, *English Rose III*, was in the mid-Atlantic, simply drifting, with the animal swimming around, quite oblivious of their presence.

Dr Heuvelmans, who is totally convinced of the sea serpent's existence, feels that more research must be undertaken, believing that a fixed underwater research laboratory will be the only means of resolving the many unanswered questions. Far from trying to prove the existence of the sea serpent, he would like to know more about their habits, the kind of food they eat and their exact life-span. Others, however, remain unconvinced as to the very fact of their existence.

3

The Woolwich Ship

During November 1912, as a result of a planned extension to Woolwich power station, construction workers uncovered the remains of a timber warship. Located about a mile down river from the former royal dockyard, it was considered at first that the vessel dated from the eighteenth century. For this reason the find seems to have been considered unimportant, her timbers being ripped out and exposed to the blazing sun. Fortunately, a number of photographs were taken, and these still exist.

The Woolwich ship, as she quickly became known, her timbers well preserved by the Thames mud, had been found 14ft below the surface. Her dimensions indicated her to be a vessel of considerable size. Although the entire frame was not uncovered, the estimated length was given to be in excess of 125ft with a width of 50ft. An obvious feature of the wreck was the remains of an enormous mast, said to be over 4ft in diameter. Resting on the keelson, the internal strengthening member that lies immediately above the keel, it was surrounded by wedges of oak bound with iron hoops. Nearby, in the hold, were found items of pottery and, presumably in use as ballast, stone shot of up to 12in in diameter.

Although, as indicated, initial thought had given the vessel an eighteenth-century date, experts were later to declare her to be much earlier in origin. If nothing else, the pottery alone was confirmed as being of the sixteenth century. One suggestion, therefore, was that the vessel discovered at Woolwich was, in fact, the *Golden Hind* – one of the most famous of all English ships. Sailing the *Golden Hind*, originally named *Pelican*, Francis Drake was to circumnavigate the world. Starting out from Plymouth in December 1577, the voyage was completed in 34 months, during which time Drake also captured the Spanish treasure ship *Nuestra Senora de la Concepcion*. Returning in 1580, the *Golden Hind* was ordered to Deptford where the nation might more easily demonstrate its obvious enthusiasm and respect for this great English mariner. In April of the following year, Queen Elizabeth herself was one of the many visitors, and it was on this occasion that Drake was knighted.

The *Golden Hind* remained at Deptford for a great many years, being placed on permanent display. In 1592, for instance, the Duke of Württemberg was taken on board, whilst official accounts indicate that a new wharf was built near her in 1624. What happened to her after 1662 is unclear, but it is generally assumed that her timbers had become so rotten that she had simply to be broken up.

Could she, then, have been the Woolwich ship? Unfortunately, the answer must be no. Not least of the reasons is geographical location. The *Golden Hind* was laid up on a site some 2 miles from Woolwich and, in confirmation of this, reference need only be made to an archaeological dig undertaken in October 1977. Partly sponsored by the London *Evening News*, its main objective was that of confirming the last resting place of the *Golden Hind*. In this they were lucky. Choosing a site close to the Pepys library, they came up with sufficient evidence to show that the vessel had most definitely been laid up in the nearby creek. Peter Marsden, the excavation director, and now of the Museum of London, goes so far as to suggest that since the c1600 levels were waterlogged, the bottom of the ship possibly still survives in the silt.

Location is not the only reason for ruling out the *Golden Hind* as a possible candidate for the Woolwich ship. Size is another important factor. Drake's ship was of about 100ft in length and only 18ft in the beam. The *Golden Hind*, therefore, was a much smaller vessel than the one discovered at Woolwich.

A final and perhaps more conclusive point, concerns design. The Woolwich ship clearly emanated from the early sixteenth century, being hybrid in character. Carvel built, there were signs of reused clinker planking. This is quite important. Clinker-built vessels — that is, where the lower edge of each plank overlaps the upper edge of the one below — predominated throughout the Middle Ages. It was a clumsy method of construction, which seriously undermined sailing quality. During the early sixteenth century, however, carvel-built ships began to be introduced, with side planks laid flush.

The Woolwich ship showed signs of both types of construction. The main hull had carvel-laid planks, smooth edged and laid end to end. Between the planks, and to prevent water incursion, caulking with pitch and oakum had been undertaken. Additionally, and one assumes it was to keep the caulking in place, a series of long batons had been placed over the gaps, creating a slight outward projection. The planks themselves also had notches cut into them, indicating that they had once been used in the construction of a clinker-built hull.

The evidence, therefore, strongly suggests that the Woolwich ship, eventually rebuilt in the carvel fashion, was originally clinker laid. The use of batons to keep the caulking in place was a short-lived idea, but introduced at a time when the art of caulking was unknown. From this point of view, the Woolwich ship bears a marked similarity to the *Mary Rose.* Early analysis of this particular Tudor warship, brought to the surface of Portsmouth Harbour in October 1982, was that she too had been rebuilt, her original clinker-laid planking having been relaid in the carvel fashion.

From all this, it appears that the Woolwich ship must date from the early years of Henry VIII's reign. Few ships of any size were built in these years, and the fate of most of them is known. However, three ships can be offered as possible candidates. First, and she can probably be eliminated straight away, is the *Henry Grâce à Dieu*; flagship of the early Tudor navy, she was, by all accounts, a beautiful ship, resplendent in huge yellow sails that were designed to represent gold. Her greatest moment came in the year 1545 when she engaged four French galleys off the Isle of Wight. It was on this same day that the *Mary Rose*, following close behind, sank as a result of an intricate manoeuvre clumsily performed.

The reason that the *Henry Grâce à Dieu* has been suggested as a candidate for the Woolwich ship is that her final resting place was, in fact, somewhere in the Woolwich area. In August 1553, whilst moored in the Thames, she was accidentally fired, being burnt to the water's edge. The Woolwich ship, however, shows no signs of ever having suffered such a serious fire and cannot, therefore, be considered the remains of this particular ship.

The second possible candidate, and the one most commonly accepted, is the *Sovereign*. Launched in 1488, she was of approximately 1,000 tons and would, almost certainly, have been of a very similar size to the Tudor warship discovered at Woolwich. Little is known about the *Sovereign*, other than that she must have originally been clinker laid. In 1495 an inventory was taken of her armament, and this showed that she mounted 141 guns. Most of these, of course, would have been extremely small, being little more than mounted hand guns. According to the inventory, they were placed on the fore- and aft-castles, stern and upper deck. No guns would have been placed below, clinker-laid planking making it quite impossible to cut gunports.

During the year 1509, and at a total cost of £193 0s 6¾d, the *Sovereign* was rebuilt at Portsmouth. It is at this time, so it is suggested, that her clinker-laid planking was replaced. In many ways, however, this does not seem to make any real sense. Immediately after her rebuilding, and probably using the same dock, the keel of the *Mary Rose* was laid. As previously stated, the *Mary Rose* was built clinker fashion, only being given a carvel-laid hull some years later – probably 1536. In other words, at the time the *Sovereign* was rebuilt, the Tudor navy was making little or no use of carvel-laid planking. If it was, then the *Mary Rose* would certainly have been built in the new fashion. Further, of course, the *Sovereign* would have retained her original hull.

If the *Sovereign* was given a carvel-laid hull, this must have been carried out at a later date. Yet, from what is known of this particular vessel, it is difficult to see just when this work might have been undertaken. Following her rebuild of 1509, she only entered dry-dock on a few very rare occasions, and then only for limited refits. In 1512 she briefly entered a specially prepared dock at Woolwich, returning again in 1521. At that time the *Sovereign*, then described as in a poor state of repair, might well have been abandoned. Certainly there are no references to her following this date. As such, the *Sovereign* might very well be the Woolwich ship. But at what precise date did she have her planks relaid in the new fashion? The chances are, they were not. And, if this was the case, the Woolwich ship is most certainly not the *Sovereign*.

A final possibility is that the vessel discovered at Woolwich was the *Great Galley*. As her name suggests, she was originally built as a fighting ship on Mediterranean lines, having an incredible 120 oars. Launched at Greenwich on 25 October 1515 in the presence of the Venetian ambassador, she was one of the largest ships in the Tudor navy. Indeed, she was as large as three Venetian war galleys, having seven heavy cannons on each side and numerous smaller guns. More important, however, is that records indicate that, although built later than the other vessels so far mentioned, she was still of clinker construction.

Like many ships of this period she spent her first years laid up in the Thames, the king having no immediate service for her. In 1522, because of a renewal of hostilities with the French, she was finally commissioned. But it was a none-too-successful début. Apparently her primitive clinker planking caused considerable problems. One contemporary went so far as to declare her 'the most dangeroust ship under water that ever man sailed in'. Because of this, and a desire to increase her sailing speed, being much slower than other comparable Tudor ships, her outer planking was completely stripped and relaid in the carvel fashion.

The *Great Galley* was to remain in service for a good many years. Her name constantly appears in the various navy lists right up to 1562. Of further importance was a second rebuild undertaken at Portsmouth in 1536. On this occasion she was converted to an ordinary man-of-war, her oared positions being removed with alterations made to the shape of her hull. At this time, also, she lost her designation of galley, being renamed the *Great Bark.*

Her eventual fate is unknown. Perhaps, sometime after 1562, moored in a quiet and secluded creek somewhere off Woolwich, she was simply forgotten, too old for further service. It is certainly a possibility. All warships, at this time, were moored in either the Thames or Medway, and usually they received little attention. It is not inconceivable that the renamed *Great Galley* met her fate in just such a way.

The Woolwich ship, however, will always remain a mystery. That she could be the *Great Galley* is a strong possibility, but by no means definite. All that can be said is that the Woolwich ship was most certainly an important discovery. Her preservation would have ranked with the current attempts to rescue the *Mary Rose.* Both vessels are of the same period and have much in common. The loss of the Woolwich ship cannot be overestimated.

4
Toll for the Brave

A land-breeze shook the shrouds,
And she was overset.
Down went the Royal George
With all her crew complete.

verse from 'Toll for the Brave'
by William Cowper (written 1782)

On 29 August 1782, the Royal Navy suffered one of its greatest tragedies. Sometime around 9.20am the *Royal George*, a 100 gun first-rate anchored in Portsmouth Harbour, capsized and sank. At the time the impact on the nation must have been immense. Over seven hundred crew members were drowned, with countless numbers of civilians, mostly wives and friends of the crew, also drawn into the watery depths.

Two hundred years later, during the opening of a commemorative exhibition at the National Maritime Museum, Admiral of the Fleet Sir Terence Lewin, then Commander-in-Chief of the Defence Staff, likened the event to a loss of the aircraft carriers *Invincible* or *Hermes* prior to their departure to the Falklands at the time of the Argentinian invasion. The analogy is rather apt. The *Royal George*, although by 1782 a somewhat aged vessel, was still a powerful element in a task force being assembled for the purpose of relieving Spanish pressure on Gibraltar.

Preparations for this eighteenth-century task force had started during the spring of that same year. The idea was that a heavily protected convoy, carrying troops and much-needed supplies, should be brought into Gibraltar Harbour, so allowing the beleaguered garrison to continue a valiant defence of the island.

44

Placed in charge of the relief force was Admiral Richard Howe whose flagship was the *Victory*. The *Royal George* carried the flag of Rear-Admiral Richard Kempenfelt, second in command.

Throughout the previous winter the *Royal George* had been held in dry-dock at Plymouth, receiving a limited refit. In truth, work upon her should have been more thorough, the vessel at that time being in a very poor state of repair. Within four months, however, hardly sufficient for what should have amounted to a complete rebuild, she was ordered away from Plymouth, bound for Channel service. A great many of her rotting timbers remained untouched, with riders being used to link and secure portions of sound timber. The attitude of those at the dockyard was that she should, with any luck, survive the following summer without too many problems.

That the *Royal George* was not thoroughly overhauled, a task that would take a year or more, results from a general lack of dockyard facilities and the need to keep as many ships at sea as possible. The war, which had started as a result of America's declared independence, was going badly for England. Since 1778 the Royal Navy had been fighting the combined navies of France and Spain, whilst defending the sea route to the colonies. It was no easy task. Nor were the various royal dockyards in a position to give any real help. Between them they had only fourteen single docks and four double docks, and were not really in a position to maintain the four hundred ships that the Royal Navy now had at sea.

Undocked in March, the *Royal George* went through the long and time-consuming process of preparing for sea. In entering dry-dock all her ballast, guns and stores had been removed together with the majority of her rigging and ship's furniture. All this had to be replaced, a process that could take a month or more. Anchored in the Hamoaze just off the Plymouth dockyard, riggers, labourers and shipwrights therefore worked ceaselessly to prepare her for sea.

In April the *Royal George* was suitably far forward to receive her senior officers. Amongst the first to arrive was Richard

Kempenfelt. Transferring from the *Victory*, his former flagship that had now been adopted by Admiral Howe, Kempenfelt brought with him a number of senior officers. Amongst them was Martin Waghorn, the new captain.

The *Royal George* herself had originally been launched at Woolwich in 1756. Throughout her twenty-six years she had seen remarkably little sea service, being laid up in the Hamoaze for the majority of these years. However, the year of her launch coincided with the beginning of the Seven Years' War, with the *Royal George* seeing a certain amount of action in the Channel. Later, as flagship to Admiral Hawke, she was present at the Battle of Quiberon Bay.

In 1761 the *Royal George* was taken out of active service. Initially it was for purposes of a refit at Portsmouth but by the time this had been completed, there was a clear sign of an end to hostilities. Instead of rejoining the Channel fleet or entering service with the Western Squadron, she was allocated to Plymouth for laying up. There was no alternative really. Maintaining such large ships at sea, the crew of the *Royal George* being no less than 840, was an extremely expensive business and to be avoided whenever possible. Such ships, therefore, were used only as flagships. Everyday routine procedures were much better performed by the smaller third-rates and ordinary frigates.

It was for reasons of her size that the *Royal George* remained in the Plymouth ordinary for the next sixteen years. With her masts removed, and her upper decks roofed over, she would have looked a very sorry sight. Certainly she would have been far removed from the picture-book image. No longer was she bristling with guns from every port nor flags from every masthead. To an untrained eye she would have been no better than any other ship held in that same ordinary — many of these no more than rotting hulks.

Her complement was also much reduced. Replacing seamen and officers were the dockyard-appointed shipkeepers. Most, of course, were former seamen, but few had the discipline that the navy normally managed to instil. Living on board the *Royal*

George, they were supposed to maintain her in a serviceable condition. Rarely did they carry out their job satisfactorily. Instead, it was merely a home for which they did nothing but keep the bilges free of excess water. Small leaks were rarely attended to, and what little equipment was held on board, unless worth stealing, was left to deteriorate.

The dockyard authorities, of course, were now in charge of the ship. Every so often she was dry-docked and surveyed, with any serious defects supposedly corrected, but such tasks were seldom performed. In 1768, six years after entering the ordinary, she was brought out for a major overhaul. Performed at a cost of £42,000, it more or less included a complete rebuild, with a great number of rotting timbers being replaced.

It was not for another ten years that the *Royal George* was again allowed out of the ordinary. In 1778 the newly declared war with France meant that every available fighting ship should be put to sea. After a further much-needed refit, the *Royal George* was brought round to Spithead for a period of service in the Channel fleet. During the next few years she was to be the command ship of a number of admirals, but mostly that of Sir John Lockhart Ross.

The war career of the *Royal George* reached its zenith in January 1781. Acting as part of an escort fleet for an earlier Gibraltar-bound convoy, she was fortunate enough to participate in the capture of two weakly defended Spanish convoys. Yet, in this moment of glory, she was also feeling her age. With only a refit since 1768, she was a vessel much in decline – a point that was to be emphasised nine months later. In October 1780, whilst sailing the Channel, her rudder simply dropped away from the sternpost.

Despite this clear indication that the *Royal George* was no longer in a fit state for continued service, she was not returned to dockyard hands for a full twelve months. Eventually, during the winter of 1781, she entered the Hamoaze for the refit that has been previously described. Referring to this work undertaken at Plymouth, Vice-Admiral Milbank, during the subsequent enquiry into her loss, commented upon the poor condition of the ship:

> When the Royal George was docked at Plymouth I had the honour to command there, and during her being in dock . . . saw her opened and asked many questions, and found her so bad that I do not recollect there was a sound timber in the opening.

Four months later the *Royal George* was again at sea. Having taken on a full complement of officers and men, she was again assigned to Channel duties before being ordered to Spithead and the new Gibraltar-bound convoy. Arriving off Portsmouth in August, she found herself one of a sizeable fleet that was due to sail during the early part of September.

On 28 August, with insufficient time available for a further dry-docking, it was decided that a limited amount of work was necessary to the lower hull below the waterline. During the recent sailing to Spithead the watercock, a brass device which drew water into the orlop cistern, had apparently become fouled and desperately needed replacing. Without this small contrivance, fitted to most ships since an order of 1779, it would be necessary to deploy buckets thrown over the side each time the decks were washed down.

Early on the morning of the 29th several dockyard workmen, including plumbers, caulkers and two shipwrights, arrived on board the *Royal George* for the purpose of fitting the new cock. First, however, it was necessary to heel the ship to port, allowing an underwater area of the starboard hull to be brought sufficiently above water. In fact, the required heel was about 7°, nothing particularly dangerous, provided the ship's movement was carefully controlled. The only real problem was ensuring that the gunports on the low side of the ship were not allowed to fall below water.

As Captain Waghorn was aware, there were several ways of heeling a large first-rate such as the *Royal George.* Undoubtedly, the safest means available was that of hauling the ship down by means of ropes attached to the upper masts and held firm by other ships in the fleet. Should something go wrong the ropes could soon be released and the heeled ship would automatically correct herself. However, it was also a lengthy process that usually required the heeled vessel to be emptied of all cargo. Instead, Waghorn chose to have the *Royal George* heeled by her own weight with heavy equipment, such as guns, being strategically repositioned. At about 7.00am, therefore, most of the port guns were run out, with a number of the lower starboard guns eased into a more central position.

Once the great ship showed signs of being heeled, the artisans from the dockyard began their individual tasks. Whilst the plumbers were actually responsible for fitting up the new system, the two shipwrights, working on the orlop deck, began drilling the necessary holes. Meanwhile, on the outside of the ship, a platform was swung out for use by the caulkers whose main task was to seal the cock in position, ensuring the vessel was watertight. From the later enquiry it appeared that none of the workmen were particularly impressed with the state of the ship. George Aynon, the senior of the two shipwrights, found both treenails* and timbers to be rotten and did not have a particularly easy task in locating timber of sufficient strength to hold the cock.

It was probably the two shipwrights who first noticed that all was not as it should be. George Aynon became concerned when a nearby table collapsed, indicating the ship's angle of heel to be increasing. He also noticed water seeping into the hold, an obvious indication that a good deal more was to be found in the bilge deck below. The majority of the crew, however, were totally oblivious of the danger. To them the heel did not appear to be excessive. Besides which, they had other things to occupy their minds. Visitors had been allowed on board, with wives, tradesmen and girl-friends all helping to create a festive spirit.

One crew member, the carpenter, was not quite so preoccupied. Viewing the entire situation with increasing alarm, he approached the officer of the watch requesting orders be given to right the ship. For his pains he received a somewhat cryptic

---

*Treenail: oak pin used to secure planks.

answer and was sent below. Eventually, unable to bear the situation any longer he sought out the captain who immediately issued the necessary instructions for the righting of the ship.

Shortly after 9.00am crew members began the task of housing the starboard guns. But it was already too late. By the time the men reached their quarters the angle of heel was so great that the guns simply fell back upon themselves. The *Royal George* was doomed.

Several gunners, aware of the imminent danger, and afraid of being caught between decks, scrambled through the open portlids. One of these was James Ingram whose escape was chronicled by Frederick Marryatt in his book, *Poor Jack*:

> I immediately got out at the same port [as Ned Carroll the gun captain], which was the third from the head of the ship, on the starboard side of the lower gun-deck, and when I had done so I saw the port was full of heads as it could cram, all trying to get out. I caught hold of the best bower anchor, which was just above me, to prevent falling back into port, and seized hold of a woman who was trying to get out of the same port. I dragged her out. The ship was full of Jews, women and people selling all sort of things.
>
> I threw the woman from me, and saw all the heads drop back again, in at the port; for the ship had got so much on her larboard* side that the starboard ports were as upright as if the men had tried to get out of the top of a chimney, with nothing for their legs and feet to act upon. Just after that moment the air that was between decks drafted out of the ports very swiftly. It was quite a huff of wind, and it blew my hat off, for I had all my clothes on, including my hat.

Ingram, and as he later recounts, the woman he pulled free from the gunport, were amongst the lucky few. Having scrambled free, they slipped along the side of the ship and into the waters of Portsmouth Harbour. Even so, survival was not guaranteed. The *Royal George* was still sinking, creating a suction effect. Ingram continued:

> Indeed I think I must have gone down within a yard as low as the ship did. When the ship touched the bottom the water boiled up a great deal, and then I felt that I could swim, and began to rise.

*Larboard: the old name for the port, or left side of a ship.

Upon surfacing Ingram found himself amidst a number of non-swimmers. Flailing out as they were, one of these grabbed his right shoe, appearing intent upon dragging him under water. To counter this, Ingram managed to kick off his shoe, whilst also pushing the man to one side. Rising once again to the surface, Ingram discovered himself close to the now partially submerged but stationary warship with:

> . . . the main-topsail halyard block above water. The water was about 13 fathoms deep, and at that time the tide was coming in. I swam to the main-topsail halyard block and sat upon it, and there I rode.

The loss of life was tremendous. With only 320 saved, the *Hampshire Chronicle* estimated some 1,400 to be drowned. Amongst this number were most of the senior officers including Admiral Kempenfelt and Captain Waghorn. Nor was death restricted only to those on board the *Royal George*. A victualling ship and two wherries, both having just put out from the *Royal George*, were also dragged down. In its description of the tragedy, the *Hampshire Chronicle* went on to give its version of the cause:

> The melancholy accident was occasioned by the ship being heeled upon her side in order to have the water pipe of her cistern repaired, at which instant of time a strong squall of wind at NNW threw her further upon her side, and the lower port holes being unluckily open, she filled and went down in less than three minutes.

That the *Royal George* was lost through a sudden gust of wind was also taken up by William Cowper in his poem 'Toll for the Brave'.

The subsequent court martial, held within a few days of the disaster, chose to look elsewhere for a cause. Rather than considering prevailing weather conditions, they looked at the poor state of the vessel prior to being heeled. Amongst others they called Admiral Milbank who indicated how the *Royal George* had been much in need of additional attention whilst at Plymouth, a fact confirmed by other officers. Also the court listened carefully to John Smart, a yeoman gunner, who at the time of the disaster had been on the lower gundeck. He told the

51

court how he had heard 'a great crack in the body of the ship'. Elaborating he went on to declare:

> She gave a great jerk, or crack, first and within a moment after another, went down. I jumped down out of the starboard stern port.

The conclusion of the court, based on this evidence, was that 'some material part of her frame had given way'. In other words, the strain of heeling the ship had been too much and she had virtually collapsed upon herself.

So far, then, two good reasons for the loss of the *Royal George*. Within a short space of time a third was to be added. This concerned the possibility that the vessel had, quite simply, been overheeled. Her lower gunports, brought dangerously close to the waterlevel, had through some terrible miscalculation become submerged, with tragic results. At the court martial several witnesses had declared this to be the case, but had been virtually ignored by those who felt that water had first entered through the heavily weakened timbers.

Despite the verdict of the court martial, there are strong reasons for considering this last suggestion the true reason for the loss of the *Royal George*. Apart from the fact that John Smart was the only surviving member of the crew to hear a 'bodily crack', the court had good reasons for reaching the particular conclusion that it did. For one thing, the Admiralty was given a convenient reason for taking a side swipe at the dockyards. The Navy Board, the body responsible for running the yards, was held in low regard. Most serving naval officers considered it an organisation that verged on the incompetent and no more than a byword for corruption. Moreover, such a verdict prevented any criticisms being levelled either at the Admiralty or its appointed seagoing officers.

If, indeed, the *Royal George* was overheeled, and this cannot by any means be considered certain, then it is likely that the presence of a rum lighter might also be an important factor. Because of the shortage of time prior to the sailing of the fleet, officers allowed rum casks to be loaded even whilst the *Royal*

On 22 June 1893 Admiral Sir George Tryon, one of the most experienced officers in the Royal Navy, gave orders that led directly to the destruction of his own flagship, HMS *Victoria*

Second-in-Command of the Mediterranean Fleet in 1893 was Rear-Admiral Sir Albert Hastings Markham whose own flagship, HMS *Camperdown*, was to carry out the manoeuvre that put her on a collision course with the *Victoria*

George was being heeled. Brought in through the open gunports, these heavy casks were then stacked on the low side of the ship close to the guns that had already been run out. It was perhaps this added weight which proved sufficient to submerge those still open gunports.

Whatever the cause, the loss of the *Royal George* will forever remain a mystery. Each of the considered reasons is highly plausible. Yet there is no possibility of discovering more. Unlike some vessels where trained divers could still unravel untold secrets, the *Royal George* no longer lies at the bottom of Portsmouth Harbour. During the mid-nineteenth century the remains of the ship were cleared. Considered a hazard to navigation, the Admiralty allowed the Royal Engineers, under the command of Sir George Pasley, to lay a number of explosive charges which were responsible for the complete destruction of the vessel. The operation was particularly remarkable as the divers, who worked on the wreck for a number of years, used an experimental diving dress invented by Augustus Siebe (1788–1872), who is regarded as the father of diving.

5

The Loss of the *Victoria*

At just a little after 3.30pm, on Thursday, 22 June 1893, two of the Royal Navy's most modern battleships were involved in a collision that should never have happened. Only a few minutes earlier, at 3.25, Admiral Sir George Tryon, Commander-in-Chief of the Mediterranean Fleet, had issued instructions that could only result in disaster. At one and the same time he ordered his flagship, the *Victoria*, together with the *Camperdown*, flagship of his second in command, to turn inwards upon one another, for purposes of reversing direction. As both vessels were on a parallel course, and separated by a mere 1,200yd, they had less than the required distance for the proper performance of such a manoeuvre. It meant, in effect, that both ships, travelling at a combined speed of 14 knots, would meet at a midway point. Destruction of one or both vessels, as was clear for all to see, was an absolute inevitability.

Those on board the other vessels of the Mediterranean Fleet considered the given instructions as representing the height of madness; a view compounded, almost certainly, by the dawning realisation that each and every vessel in the fleet, strung out in two parallel divisions, was expected to perform this identical manoeuvre. In other words eight battleships and four cruisers were all being instructed to ram one another. Once performed, and fortunately sanity prevailed amongst the rest of the fleet, the Royal Navy would have found itself totally bereft of any major undamaged warship in this most vital part of the world.

Why, then, should Admiral Tryon, a man not without considerable maritime experience, issue such an order? It is, perhaps, one of the greatest mysteries of the sea. Certainly the full truth

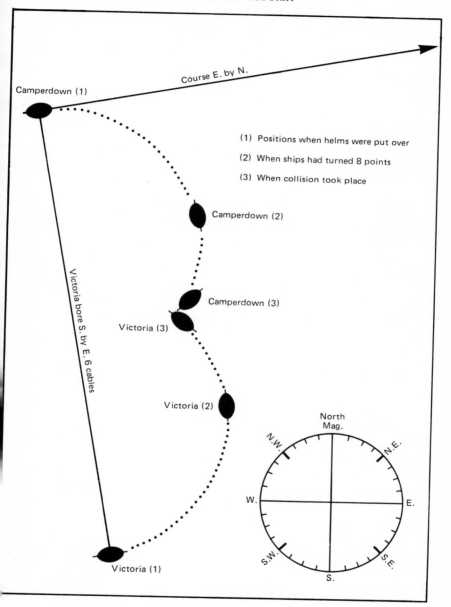

Course E. by N.

Camperdown (1)

(1) Positions when helms were put over

(2) When ships had turned 8 points

(3) When collision took place

Camperdown (2)

Camperdown (3)

Victoria (3)

Victoria bore S. by E. 6 cables

Victoria (2)

Victoria (1)

North Mag.

N.W.

N.E.

W.

E.

S.W.

S.E.

S.

will never be discovered. Amongst those killed was the only man capable of producing the answer, Admiral Tryon himself. A further question that obviously prompts itself concerns Rear-Admiral Sir Albert Hastings Markham. On board the *Camperdown*, he allowed his own flagship to participate in the manoeuvre, aware from the beginning that it was likely to culminate in the ramming of the *Victoria*. Why did he permit such a course of action? Fortunately his survival, combined with later questioning at a court martial, has at least provided an answer to this particular and just as perplexing problem.

Our investigation should really begin with Admiral Sir George Tryon. Appointed to the Mediterranean in the early summer of 1891, he began a vigorous campaign which, he hoped, would culminate in a more efficient and effective navy. The preceding years, mainly ones of peace and prosperity, had created a lethargic war machine that had become totally groomed in the fighting tactics of a previous decade. Tryon's approach to this was typical. He introduced various untried manoeuvres, each designed to instil a sense of initiative into junior officers placed under his command. This was the reason he had been appointed to the Mediterranean. Many in the naval hierarchy agreed with his ideas, and they wanted the fleet shaken out of its accumulated lethargy. They recognised him as unorthodox, and for this reason considered him the only man capable of destroying numerous outmoded ideas that had so completely permeated the Victorian navy. None considered his appointment would lead to one of the Royal Navy's greatest peacetime tragedies.

It was in January 1892 that Rear-Admiral Markham was also appointed to the Mediterranean. Directed to serve under Admiral Tryon, the two were ill matched from the beginning. Whereas Tryon was bluff, direct and inclined to dominate, Markham had a rather diffident personality which merely served to annoy his superior. During the late-summer exercises that were conducted in 1892, Markham was constantly being reprimanded for his inability to manoeuvre efficiently under a new system of signalling. In reality it was not Markham's fault. Admiral Tryon, responsible for pioneering the new system, simply failed to provide adequate time for the accommodation of his ideas. Furthermore, he was to continue in this bulldozing fashion throughout the following year. During the winter months he planned a whole set of manoeuvres, clearly hoping that his second in command, amongst others, would be fully stretched.

On 13 April 1893, a not particularly auspicious date, the *Victoria* was recommissioned at Malta Dockyard. Having undergone a limited refit, she was now ready for the continuance of her duties. Already, though, she had not proved a particularly lucky ship, a point which arose as much as anything from her poor design. A Vickers-built ship, being launched at Elswick in April 1887, she had a main armament that consisted of two 16.25in guns, each of which discharged shells of 1,800lb. In many ways it was these guns that were at the very centre of her problem. With a combined weight of 220 tons, they were the heaviest weapons ever to be installed in a nineteenth-century battleship, consequently affecting the design of the vessel. Set well forward, and in a single turret, they had to be mounted particularly low, so that their excessive weight would not lead to instability. The result was a restricted freeboard which, in anything but a calm sea, was usually awash. Of course, in such circumstances, these guns, which were the very reason for her existence, were quite unusable.

These huge pieces of ordnance provided other problems. For one thing they had seriously put back the *Victoria*'s planned completion date. Prior to being installed, one of the barrels had burst during proofing trials at Woolwich. To make matters worse, the replacement barrel was found to be so defective that this, too, had to be exchanged. Once installed, the weapons still did not prove themselves totally satisfactory. Their sheer weight and tremendous length created a problem of 'muzzle droop'. In other words, the barrels actually sagged because the carriages had insufficient strength.

As to the blast effect of such heavy guns, this was feared and dreaded by both officers and men alike. Fired forward they buckled most of the main deck and when fired abaft they caused just as much damage to the bridge. For the guncrew they were a nightmare. Most of them constantly feared that they might one day explode. This had already happened on board the *Thunderer*, a battleship fitted with similar guns but of a smaller calibre. On this ship the gun breech had become double loaded, killing most of those who worked the gun.

The fear and distrust with which these guns were regarded can best be illustrated by reference to a general belief that they were, in fact, responsible for the very high loss of life suffered at the time of the collision. Most surviving crew members believed that once the *Victoria* had begun her list to port, the two guns had completely broken away from their mountings, eventually causing the warship to capsize. Whilst it is unlikely that this happened, the sudden sinking of the *Victoria* certainly meant that more lives were lost than might normally be expected.

Finally commissioned in March 1890, by which time she had cost £817,841, the *Victoria* was immediately dispatched to the Mediterranean. In January 1892, perhaps as a future warning, the new flagship of the Mediterranean Fleet ran aground. While practising her torpedoes off the coast of Greece, she managed to hit an uncharted rock, remaining stranded for six days. Admiral Tryon had already taken command, and he was to remain on board the *Victoria* during an extensive refit that immediately followed the accident. Rarely, it might appear, was the *Victoria* out of dry-dock, and certainly she spent more time in dockyard hands than she did at sea.

The *Camperdown*, on the other hand, was a much more successful design. An 'Admiral' class battleship, she was launched at Portsmouth in 1885. Completed with four 13.5in breech-loaders, she did not have the punch of the *Victoria*, but her guns were at least more efficient, with a much faster firing rate. Before the arrival of the *Victoria*, she had actually operated as Mediterranean flagship.

On 27 May 1893, both the *Victoria* and the *Camperdown* steamed out of Malta Harbour. Over the next three weeks the two vessels were to lead their respective columns in a series of sophisticated manoeuvres, mostly those worked out by Tryon during the previous winter. Additionally, flag-showing visits were to be made to such ports as Famagusta, Haifa, Beirut and Tripoli.

At first the fleet exercises went particularly well. Haifa was visited early in June, with the two columns making their way slowly along the North African coastline. By mid-June they had reached Beirut, and it was here that the fleet remained until the morning of 22 June, the day of the tragedy. At 10.00am that morning the assembled warships weighed anchor, but it was no orthodox departure. First to leave were the ships under the command of Admiral Tryon. Steering directly between the vessels of Admiral Markham's column, they soon made their departure. Now left behind, the second division, with the *Camperdown* showing the way, began moving at a much faster pace. Soon catching the vessels being led out by the *Victoria*, these ships subsequently positioned themselves in one column, single line abreast. For those watching from the shoreline it must have proved a most impressive sight. No one else, other than Admiral Tryon, would have attempted such a 'showy' exit, and no one else would have seen the necessity. Admiral Tryon was a man on his own.

Much of the rest of the day can be traced through the log of the *Camperdown*. Steering north by east and at a speed of 8.2 knots, it was planned to anchor that evening in Tripoli. Whilst much of the day would be fairly routine, anchoring at Tripoli was expected to be a further product of Tryon's unorthodox imagination. Nothing, however, was known in advance. Tryon never discussed his plans, nor ever sought advice. It was only afterwards, when various captains were invited to his cabin that such things were ever explained. It was a point that Markham was later to use as part of his defence at the subsequent court martial:

> We used to carry out many evolutions in the Mediterranean Squadron of which at the time, I must acknowledge, I hardly knew what was the object, and they were only afterwards fully explained to me by the Commander-in-Chief in his cabin.

The fleet maintained its speed and direction until 1.30pm, at which time signal flags on board the *Victoria* indicated a course alteration of north-east by north. On board all ships it was 'make and mend' afternoon. The crews were supposedly employed upon repairing and making themselves items of clothing but, in reality, used most of the time for catching up on the latest gossip or, more simply, in resting and smoking. Officers of the watch, however, carefully observed every movement of the flagship. Anything could be expected with Admiral George Tryon in command.

At 2.20pm the two divisions were ordered to reform in separate line-ahead formations and 1,200yd distant from one another. Twenty-five minutes later a further course alteration was indicated, with the two columns steering east by north. No further instructions were received until 3.25pm, by which time the two columns had drawn level with the Tower of Lions, an old fortification being used as a visual marker. It was at this point that the final, fatal order was issued. Markham, to say the least, was surprised. His actions on that occasion were to be fully documented in a letter which was to be sent to the Admiralty just a few days later:

> As the columns were only six cables apart [1,200 yards], and therefore, not, in my opinion, within manoeuvring distance to execute such an evolution as ordered by the signal in question, I directed my Flag-Lieutenant to keep the signal, which we were repeating at the dip, as an indication that it was not understood. I then directed him to make a signal to the Commander-in-Chief to the following effect, by semaphore: 'Am I to understand that it is your wish for the columns to turn as indicated by the signal now flying?' but before my order could be carried out, the Commander-in-Chief semaphored to me to know 'what I was waiting for?' It then struck me that he wished me to turn 16 points as indicated by his signal, and that it was his intention to circle round the Second Division, leaving them on the port hand.
>
> Having the fullest confidence in the great ability of the Commander-in-Chief to manoeuvre the Squadron without even the risk of a collision, I ordered the signal to be hoisted as an indication that it was understood.
>
> On the signal being hauled down, the helm of the Camperdown was put hard-a-port, at the same time that the helm of the Victoria was starboarded.

I watched very carefully the helm indicating signals of the Victoria as the two ships turned towards each other, and, seeing that the helm of the Victoria was still kept hard-a-starboard, I directed the Captain of the Camperdown to go full astern with his starboard screw, in order to decrease our circle of turning. Seeing that a collision was inevitable, I then gave orders to go full speed astern with both engines; but before the speed of the ship had been materially checked, the stem of the Camperdown struck the Victoria on her starboard bow, about 20 feet before the turret, and crushed into the ship almost to her centre line, the fore and aft lines of the ships at the time of the collision being inclined towards each other at an angle of about 80 degrees.

The *Camperdown*, still travelling at a speed of 6 knots, caused considerable damage. More than might at first be expected. Fitted with a huge underwater ram she was, in fact, designed to inflict just such a knock-out blow upon enemy warships. And the device worked. Penetrating 9ft into the *Victoria*'s hull, the breech was immediately enlarged as the sterns swung together. The result was that once the *Camperdown* pulled free the underwater hole measured some 28ft across. Water immediately began to cascade through. Even so, the *Victoria* should still have been safe. After all, she had numerous watertight compartments, and each of these should have been closed, restricting any flooding to the immediate area of impact. Unfortunately, there had been no advance warning of the collision, and few of the compartments had been closed in time. Flooding, therefore, was soon to endanger the entire ship.

Despite a serious list to port, Tryon did not believe his flagship would sink. Instead, he considered the safest course of action would be that of beaching the vessel on the nearest piece of land, some 4½ miles away. Ordering 7 knots, the *Victoria* slowly altered course to starboard, with both engines set at 38 revolutions. The desired speed, however, was never reached. Too much water had been taken on board and within five minutes waves were breaking over the lower deck and the main guns were partially underwater. The crew, however, refused to panic. Carefully the sick were brought to the main deck and recalcitrant crew members released from the prison. All this did not prevent an early loss of life. Watertight compartments were being closed and some crew members tragically found themselves trapped in rapidly flooding compartments. Clearly, though, the reporter of the *New York Evening Post*, then at Malta, was most impressed:

> The discipline of the crew on board the vessel was perfect. The Vice-Admiral remained upon the bridge until the very last moment. Five minutes after the collision a diving suit was brought on deck, and a diver hastily put it on and attempted to go over the side of the ship to ascertain the extent of the injury. At the same instant the head of the ship was turned towards the shore, and in the ten minutes that intervened between the delivery of the blow by the Camperdown and the sinking of the Victoria the latter steamed two miles towards land. Suddenly, with a great roll and a wild plunge, the enormous vessel buried her bow beneath the surface of the sea; there were a few wild cries, the ship trembled, and then turned over with her keel high in the air, her screws rapidly whirling.

On board one of the other ships in the fleet, a young midshipman later sent this account to his mother:

> We could see from our poop deck the whole thing. The Victoria's men worked beautifully. Never, I should think, was such perfect discipline ever seen in such a trying time. We could see them evidently trying to get the collision mat over the tremendous rent. To our great surprise they made the signal, 'Negative send boats.' However, we carried on getting all our boats ready, although we presumed their watertight doors were closed and they were probably all right.

As indicated, Tryon at first did not consider the *Victoria* would sink. He was reluctant, therefore, to abandon ship, and when the order was eventually given, it was to prove somewhat late. A great number were killed by the flailing propeller blades as they desperately threw themselves off the stern, and many others were sucked under as the warship capsized. Even those farther away were not completely safe. As the vessel went down there was a tremendous explosion, with pieces of sharp, jagged metal thrown to the surface. Frail bodies were crushed and thrown helpless across the water. It was perhaps the final insult, for amongst those now endangered were the crews of numerous small boats being dispatched from every vessel in the fleet. The midshipman, writing to his mother, continued:

> Personally I was away in my boat, pulling as hard as we could to the scene of the disaster. We were a good way off, and by the time I got there, being the first of our boats, all the people had been saved by the boats of the ships which were nearer. After pulling up and down for two hours, we reorganised the fleet, leaving two ships on the scene of the disaster, and, making for Tripoli, anchored for the night. No one can realise the dreadful nature of the accident.

The *Camperdown*, for her part, was also badly damaged. Indeed, for a time it looked as if she might not survive either. There was a jagged hole in her port bow and a smaller one to starboard, whilst her stem was broken just above the bow. She, too, was shipping a great deal of water. Fortunately, though, the pumps seemed well able to pace the situation, allowing time to close various watertight doors, restricting all flooding to just seven compartments. Divers were also sent below, and they began filling some of the underwater holes with wood, whilst collision mats were thrown out. Eventually, therefore, she was in a position to be moved, being brought first to Tripoli, prior to transfer to Malta.

The news of the disaster was first released to a mortified nation on 24 June. Most newspapers reproduced a dramatic telegram that had originally been dispatched to the Admiralty by Rear-Admiral Markham. It was terse and to the point:

> Regret to report, whilst manoeuvring this afternoon off Tripoli, Victoria and Camperdown collided. Victoria sank 15 minutes after in 80 fathoms, bottom uppermost.

As always the news was hardest felt in the dockyard towns, particularly Portsmouth and Chatham. Both long-established naval communities, each had supplied large numbers to crew the ill-fated *Victoria*. With no more information as to the exact number lost, or the names, a long period of anguished waiting began. At Portsmouth, where a copy of Markham's telegram was posted at the dockyard gate, news of the disaster spread like wildfire. Numerous women called at the dockyard and fell into hysterics upon the telegram being read. Similar scenes were witnessed at Chatham, with a grand benefit concert being organised as a means of showing practical sympathy for those who had been widowed and orphaned.

To investigate the loss of the *Victoria* a court martial was deemed necessary. The accused, all surviving officers and men of the former flagship, were assembled at Malta on 17 July, ready for the court to convene on board the ageing base flagship, *Hibernia*. Amongst them was Captain Maurice Bourke, officer in command of the *Victoria*, and the man most likely to suffer in the event of the court reaching a verdict of guilty. It was his sword that was placed lengthways across the table, and it would be the position of this sword that would later act as the first indication of the court's final decision.

The day actually started with a general outline of events preceding the tragic collision. Reference was made to the great loss of life which, by that time, had been established as standing at 358 officers and men. An additional 173 were still undergoing medical treatment, mostly suffering from shock. Of the various defendants and witnesses, Captain Bourke was amongst the first to be called. Closely associated with Admiral Tryon, he was to remain giving evidence for two days. Not surprisingly he was severely quizzed as to why, with an inadequate turning circle, he allowed the *Victoria* to pursue such a suicidal course. In reply he indicated that Admiral Tryon had been informed of this fact, being told that the combined turning distances required by both the *Victoria* and *Camperdown* was 1,600yd. As Tryon had ignored this point, despite being reminded on two further occasions, it was assumed that the admiral, a recognised master of the intricate manoeuvre, had a plan in mind that was not as simple as might at first appear. Anyway, as captain of a flagship with an admiral on the same bridge, he could do little more.

A further witness, of course, was Admiral Markham. Indicating his initial concern for the particular manoeuvre, as shown by the signals, he reminded the court that initially he had refused to acknowledge the order. Finding himself reprimanded, however, he had been given little alternative but to allow the *Camperdown* to proceed on the prescribed inward turn. Markham, of course, felt most uncomfortable about the situation, but had assumed that his commander-in-chief had in mind a sophisticated plan that would prevent the two vessels colliding. Indeed, he felt that Tryon's object was to reverse the direction of the fleet by taking the *Victoria* on a much wider circle, passing the *Camperdown* on her port side. To back this conclusion, Markham called as witnesses the numerous captains of other vessels present on that occasion, each declaring that they had reached similar conclusions.

Apart from the immediate circumstances surrounding the incident itself, the court did pursue one other interesting line of enquiry. This concerned a memorandum that had been written by Admiral Tryon just a few weeks prior to the disaster. Tackling the thorny subject of discretion in the obeying of orders, it may well have been issued as part of a wider plan to test the various officers of the Mediterranean Fleet. Part of the memorandum included the following paragraph:

> When the literal obedience to any order, however given, would entail a collision with a friend, or endanger a ship by running on shore, or in any other way, paramount orders direct that the danger is to be avoided, while the object of the order should be attained if possible.

According to this, therefore, Markham, aware that extreme dangers did exist, should have taken a different course of action to the one chosen, possibly taking the *Camperdown* on a much wider circle, and so avoiding the *Victoria*, whilst still attaining 'the object of the order'.

On 27 July the court duly delivered its verdict. Admiral Culme-Seymour, president of the court, and Tryon's successor, merely read a statement which placed all blame for the tragedy on the specific order given by Admiral Sir George Tryon. No blame was attached to the crew of the *Victoria* nor, as it happens, to Admiral Sir Albert Hastings Markham. The various defendants, therefore, were free to leave the court, with Captain Bourke ceremoniously retrieving his sword. Justice had been done and, to all intents and purposes, the matter was closed – or was it? After all, the reason for Admiral Tryon's manoeuvre has never been satisfactorily explained. Many of his contemporaries were to debate the issue, suggesting a great variety of reasons for the particular manoeuvre he ordered. According to Sir W. Laird Clowes, in a letter written to *The Times*, a possible reason for the order was that Tryon intended the *Camperdown* to take a much wider circle, passing the *Victoria* on the outside. Later he elaborated upon this in his *The Royal Navy: A History*:

> For there is a well recognized naval custom which dictates that a subordinate shall give precedence to a Commander-in-Chief, and shall not cross his bows without permission, but shall go under his stern.

Another suggestion, this time put forward by Rear-Admiral Penrose Fitzgerald, appeared in Admiral Tryon's biography. Here it was suggested that the disaster resulted from a simple human error and that Tryon had confused the turning distance of the various ships involved:

> By what mental process he halved the necessary distance (or perhaps it would be more correct to say, failed to double the distance, when two columns were about to turn towards each other) it is impossible to say – though the most infallible of us must be conscious of having made similar mistakes in mental arithmetic on more than one occasion during our lives, and upon matters concerning which were really perfectly familiar as to the proper figures relating thereto. But having once got a wrong idea into our minds, there it stuck; and, looking back on our error afterwards, we are utterly unable to account for that which we properly and modestly describe as our 'stupid mistake'.

Despite all that has been written, however, none of it is anything more than pure speculation. Perhaps Tryon was testing his various junior officers, perhaps he did want the *Camperdown* to take the outer circle or perhaps he did simply confuse the distances. Whatever it was, of one thing we can be certain: on that late afternoon in June, things went disastrously wrong. Tryon, a sane and rational man, could not have intended the manoeuvre to end quite so abruptly. Nor did he intend that the entire

Mediterranean Fleet should be similarly destroyed. More than that, however, is pure supposition. As a result, the loss of the *Victoria* remains a genuine mystery and one that can never be solved.

6

The Fate of the *Waratah*

Outward bound from Durban, the Hartlepool-built freighter, *Clan MacIntyre*, was sailing on a direct course for Cape Town, eventually bound for London. Hugging the long sweeping coastline of South Africa, it would be another two days before the vessel reached her intermediate port of call. A bright but cold day, the crew were aware of a steadily falling barometer and of gradually rising winds that would eventually whip the seas into a violent maelstrom. In due course, hatches would be battened down and lifeboats fully secured. The storm, it was thought, would soon pass, but it would be a hazardous few hours, uncomfortable for officers and crew alike.

At 4.00am on this June day in 1909, a much larger vessel appeared to the stern. Recognised at once as a Blue Anchor Line steamer, she was one of a regular fleet employed upon the Australia passage. A sleek new vessel, she made a perfect contrast with the much smaller and somewhat cluttered freighter that she was eventually to overhaul. Later in the morning, as the two vessels drew abreast, messages were exchanged. The *Clan McIntyre* was the first to signal:

'What ship?'

'*Waratah* for London', came the reply.

'*Clan MacIntyre* for London. What weather had you from Australia?'

'Strong south-westerly and southerly winds across.'

As the two vessels began to distance themselves, the *Clan MacIntyre* finally added: 'Thanks. Good-bye. Pleasant passage.'

The reply from the *Waratah* was equally as courteous: 'Thanks. Same to you. Good-bye.'

Last moments for Admiral Sir George Tryon and his flagship. Rammed by the *Camperdown*, and with most of her watertight compartments still open, the vessel stood little chance of reaching port

HMS *Victoria*. Launched at Elswick, Newcastle upon Tyne, in 1887, she had two massive 16.25in guns that seemed to produce more problems than they were worth. Set well forward in a single turret, the *Victoria* was given a low freeboard to counteract possible instability. It is suggested that the shifting of these guns shortly after the collision led partly to the *Victoria's* sudden capsize

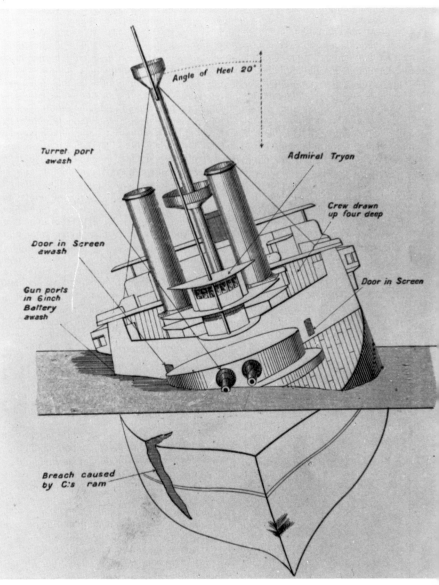

Angle of Heel 20°

Turret port
awash

Admiral Tryon

Crew drawn
up four deep

Door in Screen
awash

Door in Screen

Gun ports
in 6 inch
Battery
awash

Breach caused
by C.'s ram

Diagram of the *Victoria* on the point of capsizing

In all, the two vessels were to remain in sight of one another for a full five and a half hours, with the *Waratah* crossing abeam of the *Clan MacIntyre* at a point 13 miles from Cape Hermes and adjacent to the Banshee Estuary. When 8–10 miles ahead of the *Clan MacIntyre*, the liner was eventually lost to view in the distance.

The *Waratah*, a passenger liner that had only recently entered service, continued upon her southerly course. With 211 passengers, many in first-class cabins, and a cargo of 6,500 tons, she was fairly typical of her age. About her there was a certain Edwardian splendour, but this fell far short of the leviathan liners of the North Atlantic. Despite her comparatively limited size, she was still a vessel that should easily weather those frequently storm-tossed waters of the Indian Ocean. Even the storm which blew up some hours later, described as amongst the worst in thirteen years, should still have proved no more than a minor irritant to such a sound vessel.

Yet something did happen to the Blue Anchor Line's latest acquisition. Unlike the *Clan MacIntyre*, she was never to reach Durban. At some point, and exactly where is unknown, something dreadful and quite unexpected overtook her. No passengers were to survive and, despite an extensive search, no wreckage was discovered. The *Waratah* completely disappeared, becoming, almost certainly, the greatest maritime mystery of the twentieth century.

A Scottish-built ship, the *Waratah* was a twin-screw vessel of the 'Spar-Deck' class. Launched at the Whiteinch yard of Barclay, Curle & Co, she was soundly constructed, easily gaining her Board of Trade passenger certificate. Additionally she was built under a special Lloyd's survey, being classed 100 A1 – the highest safety rating available. Handed over to the Blue Anchor Line on 23 October 1908, she was placed under the charge of Captain J. E. Ilbery, formerly master of the *Geelong*, and one of the company's most experienced officers. Indeed, Captain Ilbery, commodore of the Blue Anchor Line, was even allowed to supervise completion of the new vessel, spending several months in Scotland.

In all, the *Waratah* was to make but two voyages to Australia, with her sudden and unaccountable loss occurring during the second return passage. Throughout this short period of command, Captain Ilbery gave no indication of any problems, nor a clue as to any potential weakness. At the end of her first passage, which actually began in November 1908, he was to declare her a comfortable vessel that handled well at all times. Certainly the first passage went reasonably well, marred only by a fire in one of her bunkers. Eventually brought under control after three days, all coal having to be removed, it was established to have been caused by inadequate insulation between the bunkers and engine-room. This was immediately corrected upon docking at Sydney.

The final and ill-fated voyage of the *Waratah* began in late June 1909. Already the Blue Anchor Line had demonstrated its faith in the new vessel, deciding upon similar specifications for a new ship of the same class. It was naturally expected that this particular voyage would result in the same level of success as did her maiden voyage. Certainly there were no problems during the first part of the return passage. Leaving Sydney with a total of 212 passengers, together with a mixed cargo of concentrates, butter, apples, lead and timber, she arrived at Durban on 24 June. A day later, having discharged 240 tons of cargo and taken on coal and water, the *Waratah* set out on the comparatively short 800 mile sea journey to Cape Town. Overhauling the *Clan MacIntyre* on the morning of the 27th, she should have arrived at Cape Town the following day. But, as has already been recounted, sometime after encountering the *Clan MacIntyre* she was to disappear completely, presumably overwhelmed by that steadily gathering storm which first registered itself that same evening.

At first her non-arrival at Cape Town did not create any undue concern. Indeed, it was initially assumed that the vessel's machinery had broken down and, once repaired, the *Waratah* would enter port. News of her supposed delay was communicated to London, with the 4 August edition of *The Times* reporting:

Were the *Waratah* a less fine steamer, not the same concern would be felt for her safety, but for a twin screw liner of over 9000 tons, built by a first rate firm last year, and sailing under good ownership, to be several days behind time is, of course, an unusual event.

Fears, however, began to increase. Even before that report appeared in *The Times*, vessels were searching the route that the *Waratah* would have followed. From Cape Town, on 31 July, the Blue Anchor Line offices dispatched the salvage steamer *Fuller*, whilst from Durban the tug *Harry Escombe* entered the search. Both vessels, though, were driven back by the heavy weather that still continued; Captain Black, master of the tug, reported that seven miles off the coast of South Africa, waves were 30ft high.

The search was next taken up by the Royal Navy vessels *Forte*, *Pandora* and *Hermes*, with all three vessels covering a very extensive area. The *Forte*, for instance, a second-class cruiser, set out from Durban on 5 August and, before her return on 11 August, covered an area of 1,320 miles. The following day she was again in the search area, this time remaining until 22 August when all three vessels were, reluctantly, ordered to abandon the search. Throughout these weeks, apart from the naval vessels, all merchant shipping travelling between Cape Town and Durban were asked to keep a look out for any signs of the *Waratah*. Nothing, however, was reported.

Only one hope now remained. There was a possibility, admittedly very faint, that the *Waratah* had been disabled at sea, her engines having broken down, and that she was now drifting helplessly outside the search area. It was noted that she had stores sufficient for three months' survival. The optimists, for instance, pointed to the experience of the *Waikato*, a steamer that broke down off the coast of South Africa in 1899. She helplessly drifted out into the Indian Ocean, being found over three months later some 2,000 miles from her original course. It was felt possible that the same had happened to the *Waratah*, so a new search was instigated. On 11 September the *Sabine*, a 3,805 ton steamer belonging to the Union Castle Line, left Cape Town with instructions to search an area bounded by the Crozet Islands to the south and St Paul to the east. She was fitted with a searchlight and was expected to remain at sea for three months. Nothing further was to be discovered, however. This rather belated search was to prove as fruitless as all the others. The *Waratah*, for all anybody knew, might well have disappeared off the face of the earth.

Intense speculation surrounded the loss of the *Waratah*, with rumours and counter-rumours abounding. Most persistent of all was the suggestion that she had been deliberately sabotaged. It was said that she had been deliberately overinsured, with the owners needing to collect the money in order to stay in business. In fact, there was no truth in such a view. If anything, the *Waratah* had been undervalued. Her total building cost amounted to £154,000 whilst insurance on machinery and hull amounted to only £135,000 with a further £15,000 allowed for disbursements. Other rumours concerned a dispute that was supposed to have broken out between the builder and owner as to her construction and that she was, in fact, top heavy. In connection with this, it is said that Captain Ilbery threatened to leave the vessel at the end of the first voyage unless improvements were made. It was further stated that both the third engineer and third mate had, in fact, subsequently left the *Waratah* for this very reason. Again, little evidence existed to support such rumours. For one thing, Captain Ilbery never officially made such a complaint. None of his letters home suggest that the vessel was unsafe, preferring to concentrate, instead, upon the more mundane matters as shipboard food and passengers carried. Moreover, the third mate, who had indeed left the ship, merely did so because of promotion.

Yet there was something strange about the *Waratah*. This, at least, was the view of one of her passengers, Claude G. Sayer. A businessman who prided himself upon his experiences of sea travel, he found the *Waratah* a most unusual vessel. At Melbourne, during the outset of that final voyage, Sayer noticed that she had an excessive lean to port with a tendency to wobble when entering disturbed water. At another time, when the weather became rough, she rolled in a very disagreeable manner, remaining on her side for an excessive length of time. Many passengers, Sayer later complained, had very bad falls. Soon after, whilst Sayer was taking a bath, the vessel rolled very much and was so slow in recovering that he had time to take note of the angle. Apparently it was about 45°. He asked one of the officers to what angle the vessel had rolled, but got no satisfactory answer. He asked whether there were any instruments on the bridge to record the angle, but understood there were not. Mentioning all this to a fellow passenger, a Mr Ebsworth who had once been a sailor, they then proceeded to the promenade deck where they observed a number of large rollers coming towards the ship. She took the first without difficulty, but when she fell into the trough she remained there, keeping her nose into the next wave, ploughing straight through it. The two men remained on watch for a long time, with Ebsworth eventually concluding that in the whole of his experience he had never seen a ship behave in such a way.

Sayer also mentioned concern expressed by other passengers. A Mrs Caywood fell and hurt both her arms and her hip, remaining in the saloon for two days. Eventually she was to leave the ship at Durban, being taken to her eventual destination, Johannesburg, in an invalid chair. At another time two other passengers, Dr Fullford and Miss Lascelles, were crossing the deck when the vessel gave one of its peculiar jerks and they were thrown to the floor. According to Sayer, this was at a time when the weather was fine, and the sea relatively smooth.

For his part, Sayer decided the vessel was unsafe. Indeed, he concluded she was top heavy. Although booked for Cape Town, with an option on continuing to London, he decided to leave the vessel at Durban. This resolve was strengthened by a strange dream that continually repeated itself prior to reaching Durban. Each night he dreamt of a man with a long sword and a blood-stained cloth, beckoning him to leave the ship. On the 28th, the possible day that the *Waratah* disappeared, he had one final dream. This time he saw the ship struggling into some huge waves. One went completely over the bows so that she rolled on to her starboard side and disappeared under the waves. At the time of Sayer's dream the *Waratah* was neither considered overdue nor suspected of having encountered any difficulties. The dream, therefore, may have been part of a final premonition, or something even stranger. Perhaps, in his dream, Claude Sayer became the only surviving witness of the *Waratah*'s fate.

At the subsequent inquiry into the loss of the *Waratah*, Sayer proved to be a key witness. He was the only person available who had sailed on her during that last voyage from Australia. Also present at the enquiry was H. M. Bennett, third mate of the *Waratah* during her first voyage to Australia. It was he who was rumoured to have left the *Waratah*, fearing that she was in danger of some calamity. According to a Mr Gibbs, the father of one of those lost on board the vessel, Bennett had told him that the *Waratah* was to be laid up for a major alteration. Bennett denied this, stating that his only reason was that he had been promoted to second officer on the *Narrung*. He further stated, upon questioning, that he had never found the behaviour of the vessel to be anything unusual. She did list in a strong wind, but this was never in excess of $4-5°$. Like her captain, he had considered her a comfortable ship, having a slow roll.

Much of the inquiry's attention was given over to the consideration of stability. Inclining experiments, conducted during 1908, were reviewed, but these only indicated that the vessel seemed to have very few problems. George Barry, chief of the scientific department at Barclay, Curle & Co, indicated that the vessel, even if lying right over on her side, had a strong righting capacity. According to this particular witness it would have been very difficult to undermine this ability, even if cargo was unevenly distributed.

Apart from stability, the court of inquiry also considered possible sighting of the *Waratah* on, or about the time of her eventual disappearance. Late on the evening of 27 July the Union Castle Line steamer, *Guelph*, whilst abeam of Hood Point, sighted a large passenger steamer. Signals were exchanged, but it appears that the officer of the watch failed to make out the entire message, reading only the letters: T-A-H. Later it was decided that this might well have been the final three letters of the steamer's name. If this was the case, and the vessel the *Waratah*, then she would only have travelled 13 miles since her earlier sighting by the *Clan MacIntyre*. As the *Waratah* was, however, a 13 knot steamer, then it would follow that she must have had an engine breakdown. More likely, though, especially as the *Clan MacIntyre* had not reported a second sighting, was that the vessel seen by the *Guelph* was just one of the many vessels to be found in the southern Indian Ocean.

Overall, because of limited available evidence, the court of inquiry was unable to arrive at a firm conclusion as to the fate of the *Waratah*. In a published report it was stated that the vessel had probably been overwhelmed during a gale of quite exceptional violence. If this was the case, and it seems not unlikely, then she would probably have been hit by a succession of waves during which time she was prevented from righting herself. Both Claude Sayer and the former third mate independently declared her to have a slow roll. The enquiry did not directly question stability, however, merely recommending that a committee be set up for purposes of examining standards of stability to be adopted by all seagoing vessels.

As for the eventual resting place of the *Waratah* this, as much as the cause of her disappearance, has always remained uncertain. In March 1911 it was thought that this particular aspect might have been solved when the British steamer *Palatina*, whilst 30 miles south-west of East London, struck some kind of underwater object. With the exact co-ordinates given as 33° 21'S by 27° 25'E, it was thought possible that this was the wreck of the *Waratah*. Unfortunately a later search failed to relocate the object. If, however, the *Waratah* does lie somewhere in this area then she would certainly have met her tragic end sometime during the evening of the 27th, and at a time when the gathering storm was still to reach its peak. Should this be the case, then it suggests that the *Waratah* was either extremely unstable, or that her eventual loss was from some quite unrelated cause. The lack of any kind of

79

wreckage, though, confirms that whatever befell the *Waratah* was extremely sudden, the ship taking everything down with her.

Along the South African coastline, interest in the *Waratah* remains extremely high. Numerous individuals have attempted searches, but have always drawn a blank. Also, quite recently, she was the star of a best-selling novel, *Scend of the Sea*, in which the author, Port Elizabeth born Geoffrey Jenkins, indicates a belief that certain weather conditions — namely severe south-westerly gales — produce valleys in the coastal waters off the Pondoland coast. Into one of these, he suggests, the *Waratah* fell, colliding, perhaps, with a seamount — a short rise in the ocean floor. An intriguing idea, and one worthy of consideration, it is certainly in keeping with this great unsolved maritime mystery.

7
Accident or Sabotage?

Imagine the Medway Estuary. On the one side, with its low lying mudbanks, is the Isle of Grain. On the other, with its ever-busy dockyard, is Sheerness. The year is 1914, and the month November. The country has been at war for just three months, with victory by Christmas now a completely dashed hope. Indeed, the German army has marched into Belgium, capturing numerous Channel ports from which an invasion of Britain could so easily be mounted.

This sudden change in the fortunes of war is the very reason that a large battle squadron should now be resting in this particular Medway anchorage. Recently arrived from Portland, the stirringly named battleships, *Implacable, Irresistible, Formidable, Venerable* and *Bulwark* are part of a fleet which is ready to resist any such maritime onslaught.

It is early on the morning of 26 November. A fresh breeze gently stirs the air, whilst the distant horizon is obscured by a thin mist. On board one of the ships, *Bulwark*, the crew has temporarily ceased work and is eating breakfast. As was the early morning custom, the ship's fifteen-man band was playing for the crew's entertainment. Moored close to buoy seventeen in Kethole Reach, the war seemed a million miles away. Some on board must have been thinking of Christmas, others of loved ones and a few of the boredom and inactivity that the last few weeks had brought. If they were, these were to be their last thoughts in this world.

At a few minutes before 8.00am all available eyes in the fleet were forcibly turned to the *Bulwark* as they witnessed an event their owners would never forget. With absolutely no warning, a great mass of flame, followed by dense black smoke, completely engulfed the vessel. A tremendous explosion was also heard, audible so it was said for 10 miles or more. At the village of Stoke, only 3 miles away, a young schoolboy, Arthur Plewis, paused for a moment in his early morning chores and looked out across the Medway anchorage. From where he stood on the road to the Isle of Grain, he could just see those ships of the Fifth Battle Squadron. At the time he did not know their names, or even why they had been brought to Sheerness. All that he knew was that they were part of an invincible navy, and one that had not suffered defeat for a century or more. On that particular morning some of his beliefs were, perhaps, completely shattered. Looking, as it happened, directly at the *Bulwark*, he saw the vessel suddenly enveloped in a cloud of smoke. He also recalls a tremendous explosion and, with the smoke clearing some two or three minutes later, there was, where the *Bulwark* had once been, absolutely nothing. Arthur Plewis, although he did not know it at the time, had witnessed a tragedy in which more than seven hundred men died in those few seconds.

Another eyewitness was Charles Drage. Midshipman on board the *London*, a vessel identical to the *Bulwark*, he was undertaking duty watch. Later that evening he entered up his official diary:

> When the catastrophe occurred I was reading a signal exercise on the port boat deck and had my back turned to the Bulwark who was our next astern.
>
> I experienced a slight shock, coupled with a blast of hot air and, on turning, saw a vast flame as high as the main truck, [a circular wooden cap fitted to the top of a vessel's mast], around which thick smoke was already beginning to form.
>
> Such debris as was in the air consisted of small objects and appeared to be largely composed of wood stored on the booms.
>
> There were two distinct explosions and then debris began to fall on our port quarter, a strong wind blowing it away from us. The place where the Bulwark had laid was entirely covered with smoke and it was impossible to ascertain the nature, extent or cause of the damage.

All around the Medway towns, and even further afield, people later recalled hearing the explosion or seeing the flash. Windows were rattled at Southend, Shoeburyness and Leigh, while at Sittingbourne a man described the flash as being 'just like a wonderful sunset'. The explosion and flash were reported some 14 miles away at Conyer, near Faversham.

Within a few minutes of the explosion a number of small craft were on the scene searching for survivors. The cutter from the *London* was amongst the first and Midshipman Drage was able to add more to his diary entry:

> By this time the smoke had entirely cleared away and the situation was roughly as follows: Ahead of us, in a straight line was the Bulwark's buoy with her cable hanging from it, the remains of her foremast protruding above water and the bows of the Prince of Wales, the next ship in the line.
>
> From the Bulwark's foremast, extending nearly to the bows of the Prince of Wales lay a circle of floating debris.

The *London*'s cutter was able to rescue three survivors from the explosion before returning. Most of the other vessels were even less successful. Of the entire crew of 741 officers and men only fourteen were rescued, of whom two later died. A number of bodies were seen floating in the Medway but the majority of *Bulwark*'s crew were clearly at the bottom of the river with their ship.

At this point the cause of the explosion could only be surmised. However, the cat was really thrown among the pigeons when the *Agamemnon*'s cutter reported sighting a periscope. At any event, the possibility of a U-boat attack was not far from anybody's thoughts and each anchored battleship, even before the periscope report, had swung out torpedo netting. In addition a number of destroyers began searching the fairways, whilst all movement on the Medway was stopped.

That afternoon, Winston Churchill, the First Lord of the Admiralty, gave the news of the tragedy to a shocked and silent House of Commons:

> I regret to say I have some bad news for the House. The *Bulwark* battleship which was lying in Sheerness this morning, blew up at 7.53am.

The Vice- and Rear-Admirals, who were present, have reported their conviction that it was an internal explosion, which rent the ship asunder.

He went on to report that a full enquiry would shortly be held.

A battleship of the 'London' class, the *Bulwark* was a product of the pre-Dreadnought era and had, in fact, seen better days. A former flagship of the Mediterranean Fleet, she had been launched at Devonport in 1899. At that time she had been the largest vessel built in the yard, having a displacement of 15,000 tons. Not surprisingly large numbers attended the launch, with *The Times* giving an estimate of 20,000. On 19 October, the day after the launch, the *Western Daily Mercury* declared that the numerous sightseers completely choked the main streets of Devonport, with traffic suspended for a considerable time:

> On all sides a perfect sea of faces presented itself to the favoured few who stood on the deck of the warship, towering an enormous height above the people, or to the ladies and gentlemen who were assembling on the raised platform, from which the actual ceremony was to be performed.

Launched by Lady Fairfax, wife of the Navy Commander-in-Chief, the *Bulwark* was soon sliding gently into the waters of the Hamoaze:

> There was a swish of rope, a sound as of heavy weights falling and striking the dog shores, and then a breathless silence. It was exactly 3.59 when the ropes parted, but not a vestige of movement could be noted for a full sixty seconds. Then almost imperceptibly at first, but gaining impetus in an incredible manner within a couple of seconds, the *Bulwark* glided smoothly and rapidly out into the water, a tremendous cheer at once going up, which well nigh drowned the screaming of sirens and blowing of steamer whistles.

At the time of her commissioning, an event which occurred in March 1902, few vessels could compete in size or power. On trials she was to give a speed of 18 knots and, fully coaled, could steam at a constant 10 knots for almost 30 days. Further, she was armed with four 12in guns, twelve 6in guns, a number of smaller quick-firing weapons, and four submerged torpedo tubes. All this allowed her to pack a fairly decisive punch, and one that was still of some value that winter of 1914.

Upon the day following the *Bulwark*'s destruction, the scene of desolation was still evident. At low tide broken steel masts, partly submerged, were visible, and there were also signs of the main superstructure. On the Isle of Grain a great amount of flotsam was being washed up against the sea-walls, much of it blown from mahogany fittings and painted furniture. Numerous people gathered on the banks, waiting to gather anything that came drifting towards them. They were not relatives of the drowned, merely souvenir hunters, or officials engaged in salvage operations. Elsewhere a number of navy divers were at work. Having been sent down to the wreck, they were supposed to ascertain the cause of the disaster. Obviously such an order was beyond all possibility. They could only report that the upper deck had been blown completely away. Indeed, destruction was so complete that it was not even possible to discover from just where the explosion had come.

The 27th November was also the first day of the inquiry designed to uncover the cause of the explosion. Held on board the *London*, one of those who gave evidence was the young Charles Drage:

> A court of inquiry on yesterday's disaster was held on board. The members were Rear-Admiral Gaunt, Captain le Measurier (Prince of Wales) and Captain Armstrong (London).
>
> I was called as a witness, and went in wearing my dirk and what I fondly imagined was a composed expression.

Drage, however, was able to add little that would help the inquiry, other than confirming that the explosion was internal. A great number of others were also interviewed, with the court's suspicions eventually falling upon the cordite. An explosive propellant, cordite was a relatively new substance and one that deteriorated under very high temperatures. On board the *Bulwark* at the time of the explosion, some of the cordite was known to have been thirteen years old, and may well have been exposed to abnormal heat. If this was the case, the court suppositioned, spontaneous combustion might well have resulted, with detonation of a magazine promptly occurring. Of course, there was very little evidence for such a conclusion, a point upon which members of the inquiry were all too well aware. In a written statement they concluded:

> It is unclear from the evidence which has been produced that the explosion which caused the loss of the ship was due to accidental ignition of ammunition on board.

The court of inquiry did, however, completely dismiss the possibility of sabotage, and this without a proper investigation. A great number of people had come on board over the last few days, these including dockyard technicians, personnel from other vessels and, perhaps, a 'foreign looking gentleman' recorded by one or two of the daily papers as having been seen at Sheerness gloating over the *Bulwark*'s destruction. That such a person existed, however, is most unlikely. Even in those days wild unsubstantiated reports were always a good selling point for a popular daily paper.

Sabotage, despite the findings made by the court of inquiry, was not as far fetched as might at first seem. German agents were certainly capable of planting delayed-action incendiary devices, with such activities now known to have occurred during the year 1915. It was during the summer of that year when the 6,200 ton *Phoebus*, an ammunition-carrying steamship, was abandoned in the Atlantic following the outbreak of a mysterious fire. Later enquiries revealed that a bomb had been planted on board the vessel whilst she had been loading at New York.

The total destruction of the *Bulwark* was only the first of five such disasters, and in each case there are marked similarities. For a start, all of the vessels were warships, and each was at anchor in a supposedly safe harbour. Kentish connections also abounded. Three of the disasters actually occurred within sight of that particular county whilst a Chatham dockyard worker, John Harston, was known to have been on board the other two vessels immediately prior to their loss. For a time, of course, he became the major suspect of an unproven crime, but was eventually released following an investigation into his background.

It was in May 1915 that the nation, once again, received news of a naval warship destroyed by internal explosion. This time the vessel was the *Princess Irene*, designed and built as a passenger liner, but since commandeered as a fast minelayer. Originally to have entered service with the Canadian Pacific Railway Co, she had only been launched in 1914. At that time the *Princess Irene* had room set aside for numerous modern features, including over two hundred lavishly equipped first-class cabins. Such luxuries, however, were to be no more than dreams, for in the early months of 1915 countless partitions were removed, being replaced by a series of trackways laid down for the storage of mines. Additionally a large minelaying port was cut into her stern. With much of this work carried out at Sheerness, the *Princess Irene*, not surprisingly, was soon moored in the Medway anchorage with a cargo of five hundred mines. Incredibly, on the morning of the disaster, 27 May, she was less than a mile from the wrecked *Bulwark*.

According to witnesses it was at exactly 11.08am that a tremendous flash was followed by the most deafening of explosions. As with the earlier tragedy, a cloud of thick black smoke soon enveloped the entire scene. Once it had cleared, all that was visible was a mass of debris. Close by, on board the *Angora*, another conscripted minelayer, Leading Signalman William Grimsby saw everything. As he was receiving a message from *Actaeon*, the Sheerness torpedo school, he had to look straight past the *Princess Irene*. At the subsequent inquiry he described seeing a flash − 'the flash seeming to come from the midship part of her' − and hearing a terrific explosion.

Another witness was Petty Officer William Wadlow. Employed upon an engine test at the nearby Isle of Grain air station, Wadlow was but a few hundred yards from the tragedy. Sheltered by the sea-wall he remembers, of that occasion, a deep internal explosion that was accompanied by huge chunks of metal being thrown into the air. Amongst items ejected was the entire deck cargo that included several hundred of the mines. These, of course, duly exploded, creating a scene that was reminiscent of some huge firework party. Where the *Princess Irene* had once rested there was a completely empty space.

According to that week's *Chatham News*:

> The force of the explosion was terrific. To many it seemed louder than the *Bulwark* explosion, and that shook many houses to their foundations. The spectacle, for a few moments, was terrific in its grandeur — one who has seen Vesuvius in eruption likened it to that spectacle for a moment. Flames and smoke belched forth in great volume. Then the flames were no more, but over the spot where the *Princess Irene* had been moored hung a dense pall of white smoke . . . not a vestige of the magnificent liner was visible when it dispersed — only wreckage.

Loss of life on board the ship was particularly high. More than 170 men were killed, among them 78 dockyard men, several ratings from a minelayer of the same squadron and all but a few of the *Princess Irene*'s own crew. Of those on board at the time of the explosion, only one man survived — Stoker Willis, who was thrown clear of the ship and rescued by the tug *Bruno*.

On this occasion, perhaps, the subsequent inquiry that was held into the loss of the *Princess Irene* came just a little closer to discovering the real cause of the tragedy. A large number of witnesses were called, and it was soon evident that, at the time of the explosion, inexperienced able seamen had been engaged in the priming of mines. Throughout this exercise speed had, apparently, been emphasised. Ratings, therefore, had been encouraged to take pistols from the storage area, placing them directly into the mines. Unaware of possible faults, one of these inexperienced ratings had almost certainly placed a defective pistol straight into a mine. Such a pistol was actually presented to the court, it having been found only a few days earlier on board the *Angora*. With a striker that projected more than $1/16$in, it was sufficient to detonate any mine to which it might have been fitted. Obviously, the inquiry could not prove this to be the case, but strong circumstantial evidence leads one to suppose this to have been the cause.

Between 1914 and 1917 the Royal Navy lost three major warships in surprisingly similar circumstances. One of these, HMS *Bulwark (above)*, destroyed in the River Medway, could have been the victim of a German saboteur *(Ministry of Defence)*. During investigation into the loss of the three warships, suspicion fell for a time upon a Chatham ordnance fitter, John Harston. In 1917, when detained temporarily, he gave his address as 2 Bankside Villas in Chatham *(below left)*. The house stands to this day. A memorial to those killed on board the *Bulwark* and *Princess Irene* is to be found close to the entrance to Sheerness railway station *(below right)*. Both vessels were moored in the River Medway when disaster struck

SAILORS, SOLDIERS, AIRMEN
AND CITIZENS.
WHO FELL IN THE GREAT WAR
1914 -1919,
AND ALSO OF
1070 OFFICERS AND MEN
OF H.M.S. BULWARK AND
H.M.S. PRINCESS IRENE,
LOST IN SHEERNESS HARBOUR
BY INTERNAL EXPLOSION
NOV. 26 1914 AND MAY 27. 19

NAVY.

H. W. ALLISON.	C. M. EVANS.
R. ALLISON.	W. H. FAULKES
L. ATKINS.	C. H. FAULKN
S. ANDERSON.	C. E. FRANKL
J. AYRE.	C. J. FURBER
F. A. BARKER.	A. S. FUTCHE
H. W. EARLING.	E. F. GEORG

THE SPHERE

AN ILLUSTRATED NEWSPAPER FOR THE HOME

With which is incorporated
"BLACK & WHITE"

Volume LXI. No. 799. | REGISTERED AT THE GENERAL POST OFFICE AS A NEWSPAPER | London, May 15, 1915 | [WITH SUPPLEMENT] | Price Sixpence.

Some of the boats attempting to push away from the starboard side of the *Lusitania* when she was beginning to heel over at a steep angle. The list developed suddenly, endangering the boats which had just been launched on the starboard side. From a picture drawn with the assistance of eye-witnesses for the *Sphere*

Of the other vessels mysteriously destroyed, two of them, the *Natal* and *Vanguard*, were both Chatham ships. On 30 December 1915, the armoured cruiser *Natal*, whilst lying at single anchor in the Cromarty Firth, was totally destroyed by an explosion which appeared to emanate from the after magazine. According to Lieutenant E. B. Turtle, then on board the *Achilles*, anchored to the *Natal*'s starboard quarter:

> At about 3.24 while looking at HMS *Natal* saw a large volume of flame shoot up from the *Natal*'s quarter deck followed half a minute afterwards by a volume of flame. These were followed by a dark yellow smoke and dull reports. About two minutes later the *Natal* began to settle down by the stern and there was an explosion along the water along the starboard quarter with dark yellow smoke. About 3.27 the *Natal* listed to port and a minute or two afterwards heeled over to port and went down.

A similar account was given by Yeoman of Signals Frank W. Foster:

> *Natal* had some flags hoisted and, as I was raising my glass to see what it was, I saw a large column of yellow smoke rise from *Natal* appearing to come from the quarter deck. I saw no water rise.
>
> I immediately reported an explosion (the sound of the explosion was very dull) and saw *Natal* on fire aft . . . A second explosion occurred immediately afterwards, smaller than the first, and then two smaller ones bursting from the port side. After these explosions *Natal*'s quarter deck was level with the water (time 3.27). Her whole quarter deck, main rigging and port waist were blazing. She commenced to heel at approximately 3.29pm

This time the death toll mounted to 390. Because the destruction was not so immediately complete, many of those on board did manage to escape. Engine Room Artificer Stanley Mattocks was one such survivor. He recounted events at a subsequent court martial:

> I was in the Engineer's workshop between 3 and 3.30 on December 30th writing a letter. I saw a blinding flash of flame come down from the marines' mess deck into the workshop. There was no distinct concussion but I heard a long drawn rumbling noise at the same time

91

as I saw the flash, and the ship's lights went out. I had the impression that an electrical cut out had blown. I waited a few moments and then finding the temperature rising, I made my way up the ladder on to the marines' mess deck, which seemed to be on fire everywhere. I made my way forward to the nearest ladder, which was then crowded by marines and others, and then escaped to the upper deck . . . It was soon evident that the ship was doomed as she started to sink rapidly aft. The officer of the watch knocked off fire party and ordered hands to unlash portable woodwork . . . The ship took a violent list to port, partially submerging the funnels. I grasped the rails and climbed over on to the ship's side and slipped down until I reached the bilge keel.

As on previous occasions, the court to which ERA Mattocks related his story was one established to discover the exact cause of the disaster. As with the *Bulwark*, progress was limited, with suspicion again falling upon inferior cordite. Indeed, some of the cordite held on board the *Natal* had been manufactured as early as September 1904, and may well have been subject to sudden decomposition, though such cordite would also have had to have been exposed to extreme temperatures in excess of 100°F:

> The court considers the loss of the ship caused by an internal ammunition explosion, and not by external explosion. The said explosion appears to have occurred in either (a) the three-pounder and small-arm magazine, or (b) the quarter-deck 9.2″ magazine . . .
>
> The loss is not due to the design, carelessness or negligence of any of the surviving officers or crew; nor, as far as can be ascertained, of any of those who are not survivors . . .

The second of the two Chatham ships, the *Vanguard*, was destroyed whilst at Scapa Flow. At shortly before midnight, on 9 July 1917, three tremendous explosions were responsible for the complete destruction of this 19,250 ton battleship. Larger and more sophisticated than any of the previous vessels destroyed, *Vanguard* was by far the most important of the five wartime losses described. Launched by Vickers in February 1909, she had a main armament of ten 12in guns together with twenty 4in guns and two 18in torpedo tubes. Even compared with the *Bulwark* she was of gigantic proportions. As to her sudden and untimely destruction, a number of very vivid descriptions were later to be given at a specially convened court of inquiry. One who was stationed fairly close to the *Vanguard* was Able Seaman John Robinson, then on board the *Neptune*. His attention was first drawn to the *Vanguard* when he saw the entire vessel bathed in a bright light. Immediately after, there was a pronounced hissing sound followed by an explosion. Two further explosions followed, these being accompanied by huge pieces of wreckage falling around him.

Most of the witnesses agreed that only a few seconds divided each of the three explosions. On board the *Bellerophon* Leading Signalman Gwilyn H. Williams also saw the same flash that had alerted John Robinson: 'The first intimation I had of anything wrong was a large V-shaped flash, almost right ahead of the ship'. As well as referring to one big explosion, Williams mentioned hearing a number of smaller reports that resembled the firing of a 4in gun on the *Bellerophon*'s own flying deck. Later the whole scene became enveloped in black smoke, making further observation impossible.

On this occasion the explosion occurred at night, darkness seriously hampering rescue operations. Numerous boats put out, but when they arrived on the scene all they could find was a large amount of floating wreckage. Three survivors were, however, picked up, but one of their number, Lieutenant-Commander Duke, later died on board the hospital ship. Of the *Vanguard* herself, nothing remained. Her twisted, crumpled hull now lay under several fathoms of water. One further tragedy had brought a sudden end to 250 lives.

Suspicion on this occasion immediately fell upon John Harston, a Chatham dockyard ordnance fitter. Engaged in machine work upon the *Vanguard*'s turret, he had also been employed upon the *Natal* shortly before that ship was destroyed. As it happens, Harston was not on board the *Vanguard* at the time of the explosion, having returned to the accommodation ship *Sandwich*. For these reasons he was immediately placed under close supervision while the Admiralty enquired further into his background. Their investigations produced nothing particularly incriminating or suspicious during the period of almost five years that Harston had been employed at Chatham. Previously he had been at Thorneycrofts, and it was with this firm that he had served his apprenticeship. Certainly Harston did not reveal any great interest in politics, and no German connections were discovered.

At the subsequent inquiry Harston was given a fairly lengthy grilling. It appears that at the time of the explosion he had been fitting and replacing Holmstrom carriers to 'A' turret, normally working from 7.00am to 10.00pm. On the day of the explosion he had left the *Vanguard* at 11.15pm. During this period of intensive questioning, Harston did manage to create some suspicion, members of the court being most surprised at the small amount of knowledge that he claimed to possess. Despite having been employed upon warships for a good many years, he knew neither the position of the magazines nor, in the case of the *Natal*, where, in fact, the magazine ventilators were positioned. Despite all this, Harston was never detained, being allowed to continue dockyard employment. Rumours, however, abounded. In nearby Inverness most people referred to an actual arrest, naming the man as 'Herman' or 'Hartman'. A few days later the First Lord of the Admiralty was questioned in Parliament, being specifically asked whether such an arrest had been made.

As in the case of the *Bulwark* and *Natal*, the inquiry rejected espionage and began looking at the cordite. One early report of the explosion, dispatched to the Admiralty within an hour stated:

> Explosion appeared to start forward. White glow seen at foot of foremast, followed by two or three small explosions, sheet of cordite flame and much cordite smoke, all of which occurred in a few seconds.

The inquiry's suspicion about cordite was strengthened when a report was received of experiments recently carried out on board the *Lion* and *Queen Elizabeth* in which it was shown that the existing system of magazine ventilation in warships was far from sufficient. It appeared that it was possible for a magazine bay to remain at a constantly excessive temperature, despite the cooling machinery, and without anybody on board even realising the fact. Further, the inquiry reported:

> . . . we find that the compartments adjoining magazines are closed for periods which, should spontaneous combustion take place in them, would permit of the temperature rising to a dangerous extent before the fact was discovered.

From all this a possible scenario was developed in which it was considered that a fire may have begun in the athwartships bunker, leading to a considerable increase of temperature in the adjoining 6 pounder and 12in magazines. Such was not a rare occurrence, a fire having occurred in this very bunker some three years earlier. On that occasion the fire was only doused when the bunker itself was flooded. Should a fire have again broken out and remained undiscovered, then temperatures in the magazine would have been raised to such an extent that the cordite would certainly have been ignited. The inquiry, therefore, went on to recommend:

> . . . that arrangements be made in all ships whereby a considerable rise in *any* compartment adjoining a magazine or shell room *must* be discovered within at least two hours of it taking place.

To a certain extent the final tragedy, in which a coast-defence ship, the *Glatton*, was destroyed by an internal explosion, went some way to vindicating certain of the conclusions reached during various Admiralty enquiries, though this was not known until World War I had ended. It was on 16 September 1918, that the *Glatton*, then lying in Dover Harbour, was partially destroyed by an internal explosion. On this occasion the *Glatton* remained afloat, but fires reduced the vessel to a useless hulk. Attempts at dousing the conflagration proving all but useless, the *Glatton* was eventually sunk by two torpedoes dispatched by the destroyer *Myngs*.

As with the four previous explosions, an Admiralty court was convened, and amongst those questioned was Commander Neston W. Diggle, captain of the *Glatton*. Although he had not witnessed the destruction of his vessel he had, of course, spoken to a great many surviving crew members. According to these collective accounts:

> The explosion undoubtedly took place abaft the funnel before the mast on the starboard side, underneath the starboard 'midship 6-inch. Eyewitnesses state that before the big explosion there were two short dull ones which caused thick heavy black smoke. Apparently this was followed by a heavier one which presumably was the starboard 6-inch 'midship shell room.

At this particular time the court was unable to arrive at any firm conclusions. It noted that every possible precaution had been taken in safeguarding the ship, and that the state of the shell rooms and magazine was normal. However, it was revealed that the boiler-room stokers were in the habit of piling red-hot ashes and clinker against the same bulkhead that divided the boiler from the magazine. Clearly, it was considered that this could have created a considerable temperature increase within the magazine. Later experiments conducted upon the *Gorgon*, sister ship to the *Glatton*, showed, however, that such temperature rises were quite insufficient for spontaneous combustion to have occurred. Instead, the court suggested, the explosion may have occurred within the area of the oil and coal, with the oil somehow becoming ignited.

Undoubtedly the destruction of the *Glatton* still remains a maritime mystery. In 1919, though, a possible solution emerged when the *Gorgon* was stripped of old insulation. Amongst discoveries made at this time was that between the 6in magazine and the boiler room, where granulated cork should have been positioned there was, instead, open spaces and folded newspaper. Additionally, boiler-room bulkheads had a number of rivets missing through which air could easily pass. From this it was suggested that the previously discovered habit of piling ashes against this particular bulkhead may, on that last occasion have ignited similarly placed paper on board the *Glatton*. Whilst the existence of folded newspaper could not be proved to have existed on both vessels, building and modifications carried out by identical groups of workmen strongly suggests the possibility.

Once such newspapers had become ignited, sufficient air would have been supplied through the rivet holes. With much of the wooden panelling soon becoming inflamed, the temperature would certainly have been high enough for a spontaneous cordite explosion.

Leaving aside, then, the *Glatton* and *Princess Irene*, since the evidence for both of these vessels strongly points to destruction resulting from an accident, it is now necessary once again to consider the *Bulwark, Natal* and *Vanguard.* For each of these three vessels sabotage immediately presents itself as a particularly attractive solution. For one thing there is the presence of John Harston who, as a Chatham dockyard worker, might easily have gained entry to the *Bulwark*, as well as later being posted to the *Natal* and *Vanguard.* Yet to carry out destruction of three ships would have required not only considerable planning, but a sophisticated espionage ring supplying the saboteur with the necessary timing devices. For this reason sabotage must be rejected. Throughout the entire war the Germans never revealed themselves capable of achieving this level of organisation within the British Isles. The blowing up of vessels leaving New York was a direct result of spies being allowed to operate freely in a neutral country. In wartime Great Britain such freedom of activity just did not exist.

Other causes are therefore much more likely. With regard to movement and storage of ammunition, all three of the vessels were very badly designed. Even relatively straightforward devices such as anti-flash shutters were omitted. It was because of this that three vessels were destroyed at the Battle of Jutland, as a result of internal explosions. The *Bulwark*, for instance, was particularly ill-planned. She had a total of eleven magazines, each connected by passageways that ran throughout the entire ship. Moreover, at both the fore and aft ends there were additional cross passages. This arrangement, therefore, was as good as a powder trail.

While the *Bulwark* had been moored in the Medway anchorage she had been taking on coal. It was customary in such circumstances for cordite to be taken down from the upper decks and stored in the ammunition passages. This had been done. In addition there were some 275 6in shells also stacked in the ammunition passages. At the time of the explosion the *Bulwark* had a large number of reservists on board. It has, on occasions, been suggested that their discipline was not as high as that of the regulars. Smoking, for instance, may well have been practised below decks – including the ammunition passages. Far more relevant, though, was the prevalence of a number of lower-deck yarns concerning risks taken by gunners on board the *Bulwark*. Indeed, the court of inquiry found some of these yarns to be true when they discovered that the cordite charges left in the ammunition passages had been removed from their protective cylinders. This was strictly against regulations.

Bearing in mind these facts we have a possible alternative scenario to sabotage. This being that an illicit smoker, be he a regular or reservist, somehow ignited the cordite. Once alight the heat of the burning cordite would explode the shells. If this scenario is unacceptable, a further alternative lies in the accidental detonation of a shell by it falling on its head. Either way, once the initial explosion occurred, the design of the ship would ensure its rapid destruction, in a similar fashion to the events off Sheerness on that particular November morning.

Whilst this series of events cannot be used to explain the loss of all three vessels, it does indicate the existence of numerous alternatives to that of sabotage. At this point, also, something else might usefully be considered. All three vessels were destroyed under wartime conditions, and it is possible that a change in routine was the factor really responsible for each of the disasters. Amongst such changes was the fact that boilers were more frequently alight and turbines constantly in use. The consequent high temperatures, often made worse by the creation of hot pockets, some of which were later discovered to exist within magazines, created a likely condition for cordite deterioration. Additionally, the constant need to keep such vessels in a permanent state of readiness required more frequent coaling. To undertake such work the entire ventilation system would have to be closed down, with numerous departments closed off. Should a hot pocket exist, therefore, the lack of ventilation would create an even greater rise in temperature. That the *Bulwark* had been in the process of coaling may not have been a simple coincidence.

Another point that leans heavily against the sabotage theory relates to the large number of vessels, mainly to be found within foreign navies, that were destroyed as a result of internal explosion. In most cases the cause was directly attributable to that of poor design, with not a hint of sabotage ever suggested. Most interesting, perhaps, concerns the destruction of the *Mikasa*, a former Japanese flagship that had been built in Great Britain. Launched at Barrow-in-Furness during the year 1899, she was of very similar design to that of the *Bulwark*. Moored in Sasebo Harbour during the night of 10−11 September 1905, an electrical fault was responsible for a fire that quickly spread to the aft magazine. The resulting explosion tore a large hole in her port side, sinking the vessel within minutes. Two other vessels destroyed by internal explosion were the *Jena* and *Liberté*, both belonging to the French Navy. The two ships were destroyed within Toulon Harbour, the *Jena* being lost in 1907 and the *Liberté* in 1912. Resulting enquiries indicated that both explosions resulted from fires having begun within the magazine. As no obvious reason would have existed for sabotage, it can only be suggested that overheating had occurred with spontaneous combustion resulting.

However, despite all the assembled evidence, the causes of each of the wartime disasters so described must continue as mysteries. The information available is circumstantial. As such, not even sabotage can be ruled out and the reader must make up his own mind. Was it poor design, sabotage or indiscipline? Whatever the cause, those who once knew, probably the ones nearest the point of explosion, are no more. They were the first to be killed. An explosion on board a warship is a terrible and hideous thing. Naturally, it is to be hoped that today's ships, sometimes carrying nuclear weapons, are somewhat safer.

8
A Mere Pawn?

Events which eventually changed the entire course of human history first unravelled themselves during the early part of May 1915. In New York, on the first day of that month, the Cunard liner *Lusitania*, was preparing to leave for her home port of Liverpool. As is now well known, this was to be her last voyage. Seven days later, and within site of the Irish coast, she was mercilessly destroyed by a single German torpedo. Although, like the *Titanic*, she was believed unsinkable, the *Lusitania* remained afloat for a mere twenty minutes, during which time only a small fraction of her crew and passengers managed to escape.

Although not directly responsible for America's entry into World War I, the sinking of the *Lusitania* with a large number of US citizens on board is generally believed to have had an important influence upon President Wilson. Certainly the British Government made much of the issue, determined to exploit one further German atrocity. In the months that followed little press attention was given to counter claims that the liner not only carried an extensive cargo of munitions but, at the same time, was armed. Additionally, both in 1915 and more recently, it has been suggested that the *Lusitania*, being without any form of naval escort, was deliberately allowed to enter U-boat infested waters. According to this view, members of the Admiralty pursued such a stratagem, confident that should she be sunk, then an alliance with the USA could be expected.

If this last be correct and the *Lusitania* was no more than a pawn, sacrificed in the name of war, then the man moving her was no less a personage than Winston Churchill, then First Lord of the Admiralty. A politician of considerable experience, appointed to the post some two-and-a-half years earlier, he had since the outbreak of war been responsible for a number of schemes designed to influence President Woodrow Wilson into a pro-allied stance. Indeed, only six weeks prior to the sinking of the *Lusitania* he had actually written to fellow cabinet minister Walter Runciman (later Lord Runciman), expressing his views on the matter:

> My Dear Walter, it is most important to attract neutral shipping to our shores, in the hope especially of embroiling the U.S. with Germany. The German formal announcement of indiscriminate submarining has been made to the United States to produce a deterrent effect upon traffic. For our part we want the traffic — the more the better and if some of it gets into trouble, better still.

Indeed, this appears to have been exactly what happened. In February 1915 Germany had declared the waters around Great Britain a war zone in which all vessels were liable to attack. Apart from the *Lusitania*, certain American vessels were also torpedoed, creating considerable pro-British feeling in the USA. From this point of view, therefore, it was a very neat plan, and one in which Churchill was seemingly involved from the outset.*

Whether at the centre of high-level intrigue or not, the *Lusitania*, during the process of boarding passengers at New York's famous pier 54, was already the attention of much speculation. In various American newspapers, perhaps as many as fifty in number, advertisements had appeared, each warning intending passengers that they were in great danger. Although not mentioning the liner by name, the positioning of these notices, always as close as possible to Cunard's own sailing announcements, left little room for doubt. Issued as they were by the German Embassy, they declared that 'vessels flying the flag of Great Britain, or any of her allies' were liable to destruction. Appearing to some as nothing more than an amateurish attempt

---

*In his own account of the war, Winston Churchill, in writing *The World Crisis* (1923), declared of this stage of the war: 'The first German U-boat campaign gave us great assistance . . . It altered the whole position of our controversies with America. A great relief became immediately apparent.'

at intimidation, it was seen by others as a clear sign of a premeditated German plot. Whatever the reasons, however, a number of passengers did cancel, their lives saved by this particular German contrivance.

Further warnings to intending passengers were also issued, this time taking the form of telegrams. Addressed to a number of first-class passengers, each referred to great dangers ahead. Amongst such recipients was millionaire sports enthusiast Alfred G. Vanderbilt, then travelling to England in connection with a number of horse shows he was in the process of arranging. Never to arrive at his hoped for destination, he was amongst hundreds later drowned in the waters off the Old Head of Kinsale. The telegram sent to him simply read: 'Have it on definite authority the Lusitania is to be torpedoed. You had better cancel passage immediately'. Emphasizing the point, the telegrams was menacingly signed *morte.*

That this voyage of the *Lusitania* might well result in tragedy was a possibility also being fostered by a great number of newspapers. Journalists from the popular press were certainly on hand that morning, desperate for interview material and comment. Of those prepared to oblige, Alfred Vanderbilt was amongst the most forthcoming. Always one for the limelight, and recognizable by a tweed cap and smart double-breasted, charcoal-grey suit, he firmly announced that, despite his telegram, he had little fear for his own life. To one gossip columnist he went on to declare: 'Why should we be afraid of German submarines? We can out distance any submarine afloat.'

Of the other passengers, most seemed to share Vanderbilt's belief. Certainly a large number realized that no German U-boat had a speed in excess of the *Lusitania.* Indeed, the Cunard passenger liner was a one-time holder of the Blue Riband, having achieved only a few years earlier the fastest crossing of the Atlantic. With a known speed, therefore, of 26 knots, she was considered well able to avoid any likely pursuit. Admittedly, as a wartime economy, a number of her boilers had been shut down, a point not freely admitted by Cunard, but even so she could maintain a speed that was nearly twice that of any submerged U-boat. Her only danger, and one assumes that this had not occurred to any of her passengers, was that the attacking submarine was already positioned, the huge liner then being the perfect target.

Apart, therefore, from a great number of passengers, another of those unperturbed by various threats was the ship's captain, William Thomas Turner. A senior officer of the Cunard Line, holding the position of commodore, he was a highly experienced seaman who had served an apprenticeship on a wide variety of vessels. Earlier commands had included both the *Mauretania* and *Aquitania*, whilst he had steered the *Lusitania* to at least one of her Blue Riband successes. Now a man close to retirement, he looked forward to an uneventful passage with an early docking at Liverpool. As was the custom, he had that same morning reported to the British Consulate where he had been informed of a rendezvous point with the Royal Navy warship HMS *Juno*. Not a very satisfactory choice, the *Juno* being a rather ageing cruiser, her presence would, nevertheless, be of some value, submarines rarely attacking when a patrol boat was in the vicinity. Captain Turner also learnt during his visit to the consulate, the true extent of the current U-boat campaign. He was told that earlier the same day, for instance, an attack had been carried out upon the US tanker *Gulflight*. One torpedo had been sufficient to dispatch the vessel which, at the time, had been a few miles off the Isles of Scilly. Soon the *Lusitania* herself would be in nearby waters, her work cut out to avoid this every-growing threat.

Eventually, at 12.30pm on that May Day afternoon the *Lusitania* was slowly eased from that familiar New York pier. As always, hundreds of spectators lined the shore, many attracted by the day's events and frequent predictions of a likely tragedy. Effortlessly the four stacker headed down the Hudson River, aided by three tugs. Who, on that day, could really conceive of anything happening to that leviathan of the seas? Nothing less than a floating hotel, she was one of the finest ships that had ever entered New York harbour. The first seagoing vessel to exceed

30,000 tons, her proportions were truly staggering. Almost as tall as St Paul's Cathedral her great length, exactly 787ft, was sufficient to stretch the length of this same building one-and-a-half times.

Size, however, was only one of several reasons that the *Lusitania* was famed throughout the world. Within engineering circles her various technical innovations were renowned, leading to immense changes having to be made in all later passenger liners. Of these, the adoption of the steam turbine engine was the most revolutionary, the *Lusitania* having abandoned the much-tried and tested reciprocating machinery with which she might normally have been fitted. Apart from this, she was also the first passenger ship to be equipped with internal passenger lifts, whilst it should also be noted that the *Lusitania* was electrified throughout and had an early form of air conditioning. As for accommodation this was of a particularly high standard, with dining-rooms, writing- and smoking-rooms nearly always adopting the style of a former age. Thus first-class passengers, having dined in surroundings heavily influenced by the reign of Louis XVI, could retire to a Georgian-decorated lounge or Adam-style library. Second-class passengers were also treated to a similar extravagance, most of their rooms also being of the eighteenth century. Third-class passengers, however, crowded into a much smaller space, found the centrepiece of their accommodation to be a rather simple squat dining-room supported mostly by undecorated columns and rather plain walls. Few, though, would have complained since the standard was much higher than that generally offered by other liners that then plied the various Atlantic routes.

Following the excitement of New York, with its hounding of intending passengers by newspaperman, the Atlantic crossing was to prove somewhat tedious. Deck games, as always, were a central attraction, but marred by the all-engrossing fear of submarine attack. For this reason passengers took longer than normal to settle, several not even bothering to unpack. Captain Turner was certainly aware of this mood, and it perhaps influenced him in his failure to call a lifeboat drill for passengers. Yet he was certainly not ignoring the German threat. He, more than anyone else, knew of the likely dangers, taking a number of obvious precautions. Amongst other things, portholes were secured and blacked out, whilst the majority of watertight bulkheads were closed. Additionally, as the liner neared those waters around the British coastline, all the lifeboats were swung out, ready at a moment's notice, and the various watches doubled.

Responsible for the eventual destruction of the *Lusitania* was the U-20 which, by any standards of the sea, was nothing less than a minnow. Whereas the *Lusitania* could boast herself amongst the fastest and greatest, this particular German U-boat was amongst the slowest and perhaps least significant. Of 210½ft in length and with a draught of only 11ft, her operating range was less than 5,000 miles. Yet, armed with seven G-type torpedoes, she was also a threat to any warship or passenger liner afloat. Noisy, uncomfortable and dangerous, her crew were forced, for hours on end, to live huddled together in what was nothing less than a tiny, stinking tin can. The difference between the U-20 and the luxury of the *Lusitania* could not be more apparent.

Commanded by Kapitanleutnant Walther Schweiger, the tiny U-20 had been at sea one day longer than the *Lusitania*. Having put out from Emden on 31 April Schweiger was in receipt of orders that allowed him to attack enemy shipping found both within the Channel approaches and the newly declared war zone. These specific instructions were directed to a number of submarines of the Third Flotilla:

> Large English troop transports expected starting from Liverpool, Bristol (south of Liverpool), Dartmouth . . . get to stations on the fastest possible route around Scotland; hold them as long as supplies permit . . . submarines are to attack transport ships, merchant ships, warships . . .

Schweiger's route from the Baltic, therefore, was long and tedious, with the submarine eventually reaching the south coast of Ireland some six days later. Successful attacks were then carried out upon the schooner *Earl of Lathom* and two merchant steamers of the Harrison Line, the *Candidate* and *Centurion*. All took place within a period of twenty-four hours with each vessel destroyed in an area bordered by Kinsale and St George's Channel. Clearly, therefore, the Admiralty had been notified of the existence of a U-boat and, even more important, one that was in the direct path of the *Lusitania*. Their response, and this point is crucial, was not so much to warn the *Lusitania* but instead to remove the *Juno* from her patrol area. Captain Turner and his near two thousand passengers and crew were now on direct course for the U-20, denied that small additional protection that might have been afforded by the *Juno*.

Friday 7 May was the liner's last fateful day. Crew members on board the German submarine first became aware that the liner was approaching sometime in the early afternoon. Initially represented by nothing more than a speck of black smoke on a very distant horizon, her massive proportions did not become immediately obvious. Eventually, however, with numerous binoculars trained upon her, the unmistakeable silhouette was to provide little doubt as to her identify. Four stylishly raked funnels set on a white gleaming superstructure left small room for doubt. The ship must be the *Lusitania*; no other Cunarder four-stacker could possibly be in this same area. As for Schweiger's reaction, this was to prove predictable. He had little choice, the vessel now before him had to be sunk. In common with all other U-boat commanders he firmly believed that she was involved in the munitions trade. Below decks, shielded by a cargo of rich passengers, was the real target — munitions bound for Europe. These must be destroyed; all other factors were immaterial.

Yet, unprotected as she was, being without mounted guns and naval escort, the *Lusitania* would be no easy target. Although on a course that brought her much closer, the U-20 would still be out of range. Aware of this, Schweiger ordered an immediate alteration of course, the object being that of positioning the U-boat for a torpedo attack at maximum range. As such, the chances of any kind of success were minimal. That is, until the

Of various mysteries connected with the Bermuda Triangle, few equal the strange disappearance of the USS *Cyclops* (*US National Archives*)

A rare picture of the M.1, depicted during a courtesy visit to Venice. Armed with a huge 12in external gun, often making her difficult to control, it was this which was at first thought to have caused her loss (*RN Submarine Museum*)

Lusitania also altered course, turning even more directly towards the submarine. For the commander of the U-boat it was a moment for jubilation. The two vessels were now closing, allowing the submarine the chance of a perfect bow shot. At exactly 2.10pm, therefore, one small G-type torpedo, fitted with 290 tons of TNT, was despatched on its course. Having been given a delayed time fuse, it would only explode after maximum penetration.

Fifty seconds later all hell was let loose. On board the U-20, submerged since the *Lusitania* had first been sited, the sounds of an explosion were clearly audible. The liner had been hit. The torpedo, travelling at a speed of forty knots had slammed into the starboard side, entering deep into one of several coal bunkers positioned immediately behind the bridge. The resulting damage should, nevertheless, have been limited. But this was not the case. Less than a minute later a further and even louder blast was also heard. Something else had also exploded. Watching events through his periscope, Schweiger dictated an entry for his log book:

> An unusually heavy detonation takes place with a very strong explosion cloud far beyond the front funnel. The explosion of the torpedo must have been followed by a second one − boiler − or coal − or powder? The superstructure above the point of impact and the bridge are torn asunder, fire breaks out, smoke envelopes the high bridge.

It was this second explosion which caused most of the damage. As noted by later exploration of the wreck, a massive hole had also been torn into the port side of the vessel, forward of the first funnel. Allowing thousands of tons of water to enter the vessel, there was no way the *Lusitania* could remain afloat. Within minutes she was suffering a 15° list that also caused considerable problems for the launching of the lifeboats. Those on the port side, now swinging well away from the hull, were impossible to board, whilst on the starboard side they were simply hanging over the decks. Attempts to move these boats often resulted in tragedy, with a number of them, loaded with sixty people or more, crashing down on to assembled groups below.

The launching of lifeboats was only one difficulty. Although panic was generally avoided, a number of passengers on the lower decks found themselves trapped by steadily rising water levels. Hundreds made for the stairs and lifts, desperately trying to reach the higher decks. Of these, a few were fortunate, able to reach the promenade and boat decks, only to discover the problems that had arisen in launching the lifeboats. Some, those who could swim, had little alternative but to throw themselves overboard; others, lacking this ability, remained where they were and awaited the turn of events. Perhaps the least fortunate were those who had entered the lifts. It was the worst thing they could have done. Within minutes of the attack all electricity throughout the ship dramatically failed, with those inside the lifts helplessly trapped. Nothing could be done for them, their desperate pleas for help going completely unanswered.

In the radio cabin the telegraphists were already at work. Without instruction, but well aware that the ship was in difficulties, the senior officer, Robert Leith, was sending out a desperate message. The internationally recognized SOS was followed by the *Lusitania*'s call sign and position: 'Come at once. Big list ten miles south Old Head Kinsale.' Despite a transmitter rapidly losing power, the message was picked up far and wide. A number of merchantmen immediately made for the stricken vessel, whilst a number of warships based in Cork Harbour were also ordered to fire up and steam out. Amongst the latter, and somewhat ironic given the circumstances, was the *Juno*, the cruiser that had once been destined to provide the *Lusitania* with protection against attack.

The first of the rescue ships did not begin to arrive until several hours had elapsed. Nearest to the scene of the tragedy was the Glasgow trawler *Peel 12*. No more than a small sailing vessel, she was hopelessly becalmed under the Head of Kinsale and almost within sight of the liner. Other vessels were much further off, whilst those in Cork Harbour had to spend some time in raising steam. Nevertheless, sailors on board any vessel within reasonable distance did their utmost to reach the stricken Cunarder. But on arrival there was little they could do. The *Lusitania* had long since slipped below the waves, a high proportion of passengers going down with her. For the rescue craft, therefore, all that was left was a full scouring of the area, searching out survivors who, in most cases, were found clinging to small pieces of wreckage. A few, of course, had managed to get away in lifeboats, but by then most had reached the shore. The death toll, not fully known until some weeks had elapsed, was eventually to reach the awful figure of 1,201; it represented two-thirds of those who had boarded the vessel in New York.

A terrible deed, therefore, and one of quite bestial proportions, the sinking of the *Lusitania* was soon at the centre of a massive propaganda campaign. Fermented by the British Government, it was mostly directed towards the American mainland and its neutralist president. As might be expected, the Germans were soon on the defensive, their claims that the liner was a legitimate target being rapidly dismissed. Newspapers in particular took up the allied cause, providing their readers with long detailed descriptions of the slaughter that had taken place, many dwelling on the fact that 128 American lives had also been lost. Most called upon President Wilson to take immediate action, with not a few suggesting that war was the only real solution. Certainly in their condemnation of the act, newspapers throughout the length and breadth of the United States spoke as one. In the pages of the highly respected *Journal of Commerce*, readers were informed that: 'The attack on the 'Lusitania' was not war, it was simply attempted murder on a scale deliberately intended to inspire general consternation and fear'. The *Philadelphia Public Ledger* was a little more reserved, declaring in its 8 May issue: 'The utter recklessness of the German submarine campaign against merchantmen, beligerent or neutral, reaches its appalling climax in the reported sinking of the 'Lusitania'. In New York, the *Tribune* simply screamed: 'For this murder there is no justification'. As for the *Richmond Times-Despatch*: 'Germany surely must have gone mad'. Whilst *The Nation* called it, '. . . a deed for which a Hun would blush, a Turk be ashamed, and a Barbary Pirate apologize'. Anti-German riots were inevitable.

In many respects the German Government was extremely fortunate that war remained undeclared for the time being. Certainly America's 'Joe Public' would have been in sympathy, the mind of the nation having been carefully manipulated by a largely pro-Allied press. Also, of course, a number of leading politicians were demanding war, amongst them the former president Theodore Roosevelt. For Woodrow Wilson it must have appeared as if he was the only man in the United States who did not wish to go to war. Instead, he gave the matter careful and deep consideration, determining upon the submission of a diplomatic protest couched in the very strongest language. Noting the deaths of so many Americans, he reiterated the right of all such citizens to travel the high seas unmolested, charging the Germans with 'strict accountability'. To the citizens of Philadelphia on 10 May he outlined some of his reasons for such a move:

> The example of America must be the example not only of peace because it will not fight, but of peace because peace is the healing and elevating influence of the world and strife is not. There is such a thing as being too proud to fight.

Outwardly, then, this was the situation that prevailed in May 1915. More recent evidence, however, shows the whole matter to have been a lot more complicated. For one thing, it appears that President Wilson considered the *Lusitania* to have been no ordinary liner. He possessed a wealth of evidence to show that not only was she under direct Admiralty orders, but that she carried a massive cargo of munitions. In believing this, the American president could only conclude that passengers on board the ship were being ruthlessly used to protect the vessel from attack. That the Germans had subsequently ignored the existence of these passengers did not make the British Government any less guilty. For this reason, hostilities with the German nation could not be considered. In his eyes, both sides were equally blameworthy,

112

with neither deserving his favour in such an important matter as that of war.

So, it must be asked, was the *Lusitania* running contraband? As might be expected, the details are still very much clouded in a heavy mist of secrecy. The British Admiralty, for its part, continues to deny any such suggestion. As far as they are concerned the *Lusitania* was nothing more than an innocent victim of an unprovoked U-boat attack. But, in reality, such a position can no longer be substantiated. Too much evidence now exists to the contrary. For one thing, there is the ship's manifest which was delivered to President Wilson immediately after the sinking. Submitted originally to US customs officials, it shows quite clearly that amongst declared cargo on board there existed 4,200 cases of cartridges and 1,259 cases of steel shrapnel. On top of this, however, certain other items on this manifest, including 3,863 boxes of cheese and 696 tubs of butter have to be viewed with a certain suspicion. Although it is not known where they came from, their destination is certainly known – this being none other than the Naval Experimental Establishment at Shoeburyness.

Added details as to the cargo carried by the *Lusitania* have mostly been uncovered by journalist and academic Colin Simpson whose book, *Lusitania*, was first published in 1972. Amongst other things he expresses his belief in the fact that all of the cargo holds had been commandeered by the Admiralty and subsequently loaded with what could only be considered as contraband. Furthermore, and this is something else that Simpson considered more than feasible, was that the second explosion witnessed by Kapitanleutnant Schweiger was in fact part of this illicit cargo.

It was in the summer of 1982 that the theory of the cargo exploding received dramatic support. In that year a specially organized salvage team began an investigation of the wreck that included the use of a remote controlled submarine fitted with underwater cameras. Undertaken by Oceaneering Ltd, but supported by both the BBC and *Sunday Times*, members of the team had little difficulty in finding the wreck. Situated some thirteen miles off the coast of Ireland and in 320ft of water, the remains looked not unlike a giant scrapyard. Crumpled metal and sheered plates were strewn everywhere, whilst the superstructure of the liner had apparently collapsed many years earlier. More or less intact, however, was the hull, and it was here that a number of startling discoveries were made. Instead of being just one hole, the submarine's camera detected a second hole in the port side. Far too large to have been created by a torpedo it must have resulted from a much greater explosion, probably a quantity of ammunition which Simpson indicates to have been stored in this area. Unfortunately the salvage team was unable to produce further evidence as to the existence of munitions being carried, the original cargo having been removed at an earlier date. This possibly occurred in 1954 when the *Reclaim*, a large recovery ship fitted with a cargo grab, was brought to the wreck whilst under Admiralty contract.

Another point of controversy surrounding the *Lusitania*, and which might also have influenced President Wilson, was the possibility that she had actually been armed at the time of the attack. Outwardly a rather unusual suggestion, it is not beyond the realms of possibility. After all, the building of the *Lusitania* was actually financed by the Admiralty, the liner being designed to serve as an armed cruiser in the event of war. Admittedly, during the period leading up to her last voyage, none of the passengers or crew ever admitted to seeing such guns, but these would have been securely hidden in one of several coal bunkers.

As a passenger liner the *Lusitania* was originally laid down in February 1905. A massively expensive undertaking, it is unlikely that Cunard would have gone ahead with the vessel unless the Admiralty had agreed to underwrite the entire building costs. In return, however, Cunard had not only to agree that the vessel would always be available for naval use, but also that her design would be more suited to that of a warship. For this reason the *Lusitania* was completed with, amongst other things, engines and boilers below the waterline, placed there for greater safety. More important, however, was the fact that she was also provided with sufficient room for the eventual mounting of twelve 6in quick-firing guns. To be mounted on the shelter deck, promenade deck and beneath the promenade deck, these guns, once installed, were to be served by ammunition hoists and separate magazines. Details of the arrangement were subsequently published in the 2 August 1907 edition of the journal *Engineering*:

> For purposes of attack the Lusitania will be provided with an armament as satisfactory as the armoured cruisers of the County class, because on one of the topmost decks there will be carried, within the shelter of the heavy steel plating, four 6 inch quick-firing guns, attaining a muzzle energy of over 5,000 foot tons, while on the promenade deck on each side there will be four more guns on central pivot mountings, also able to penetrate 4¾ inch armour at 5,000 yards range, and 6 inch armour at 3,000 yards range.

At that time neither guns, magazines nor shell lifts were actually fitted to the *Lusitania*, this being planned for a future date. In 1913, with the chances of war becoming ever more likely, the Admiralty took up its option on the liner, ordering her to be dry-docked at Liverpool. It was then that the magazines were fitted together with revolving ring mounts for the guns. Attempts by the Admiralty to conceal the reasons for the *Lusitania*'s docking completely failed with the New York *Tribune* of 19 June 1913 calling attention to the fact:

> The reason why the crack liner *Lusitania* is so long delayed at Liverpool has been announced to be because her turbine engines are being completely replaced, but Cunard officials acknowledged to the *Tribune* correspondent to-day that the greyhound is being equipped with high power naval rifles in conformity with England's new policy of arming passenger boats. So when the great ship . . . next appears in New York Harbor about the end of August she will be the first British merchantman for more than a century sailing up the Lower Bay with her guns bristling over the sides.'

As it happens the guns themselves were not fitted at this point in time. Although ordered they did not arrive in Liverpool until November. Additionally, even if they had been ready they would not have been 'bristling over the sides' as the mountings were not permanent. Instead, the guns were to be held below deck and brought to the mountings only when needed. Special bolts and other attachments were supplied for the purpose, their fitting into place taking a mere twenty minutes.

With the guns available, but held in store, the *Lusitania* was very close to being a warship. In August 1914 she underwent the final stage, again being docked in Liverpool. On this occasion the guns were actually installed, whilst her cargo holds were generally enlarged. By September, therefore, she was, in truth, a heavily armed warship, carrying more guns than the average cruiser. Because of this she would have been destined for patrol duties in the South Atlantic, but a sudden change in Admiralty thinking saw her returned, instead, to Cunard. Apparently, so it was now felt, she would be far more useful in the continuing role of passenger liner, her enlarged cargo holds available for the transportation of American-manufactured armaments. As for the 6in guns, nobody appears to know their eventual fate. Having already been brought on board, it seems unlikely that they would have been removed.

The third and final controversy connected with the *Lusitania* concerns the suggestion that she was deliberately endangered, with the idea that any possible U-boat attack would lead to American involvement in the war. Not surprisingly, it was a number of German community newspapers in America that first raised this possibility. Understandably they failed to see why the *Lusitania*, completely without escort, should have been allowed to enter a declared war zone. *The Fatherland*, published in New York, gave much attention to statements made by Richmond Pearson Hobson, a former member of the House of Representatives. Apparently he had been advised by a Cunard official, a long-time friend of the family, that he should not reserve passage on the boat, it being said that warnings had been received from the British Admiralty as to her likely destruction. The 26 May edition went on to report a note that Pearson had sent to President Wilson in which he declared that Germany had no motive for desiring to destroy the lives of the 128 American citizens on board. Instead, he insisted, such motives would be more appropriate for Great Britain who wished to see the United States becoming embroiled in the European war.

As indicated earlier, if the *Lusitania* was being ordered to her destruction, then one man who would automatically have been involved was the then First Lord of the Admiralty, Winston Churchill. An enthusiastic member of the War Cabinet, the majority of Churchill's activities were directed towards bringing about a successful and swift end to the war. As First Lord he was noted for a number of spectacular enterprises in which naval warships were often seen as expendable. Amongst other things, he was the first to advocate the bombing of military targets inside towns and pushed for the use of poisoned gas at Gallipoli. The gambling of a few hundred lives on board a passenger liner may well have seemed nothing when set against the possibility of shortening the war by several months, or even years.

The evidence, however, is based on nothing more than circumstance and supposition. Apart from Churchill's letter to Walter Runciman, written in February 1915, the other strongest piece of evidence concerns the First Lord's presence at the Admiralty on 5 May. This was the day that the *Juno* was withdrawn from her patrol area, leaving the *Lusitania* to enter the war zone without any form of protection. Officially it was stated that the *Juno* would be in danger herself, also a likely target for attacking U-boats. But nothing was done about the *Lusitania*, the even bigger target that the *Juno* should have been helping to protect. Instead a large and vulnerable passenger liner, already threatened with attack whilst at New York, was approaching the coast of Ireland, steaming on a course that would take her straight into the path of a hostile U-boat whose whereabouts was known to the Admiralty. Surely this, in itself, says something. Either the First Lord was pursuing his plans as revealed to Runciman, using American citizens in place of neutral ships, or he was responsible for an act of extreme neglect.

Admittedly, the sinking of the *Lusitania* did not result in an immediate American entry into the war, but it did pave the way for her future participation. In the meantime a distinct softening of American criticism towards the allies was clearly discernible. It was a point that Churchill himself made some twenty-two years later in an article written for the *News of the World*: 'The poor babies who perished in the ocean struck a blow at the German power more deadly than could be achieved by the sacrifice of a hundred thousand fighting men'.

That the possible hazarding of the *Lusitania* counts as the final controversy is because it is a matter that will never fully be resolved. After all, it must now be accepted as a virtual certainty that the liner was involved in the carrying of munitions, whilst the existence or non-existence of guns is likely to be verified by the eventual release of relevant Admiralty papers. But this will never be the case as to whether the *Lusitania* was being used as 'live bait'. The trouble with such an accusation is that it relies upon an unrecorded discussion that might have taken place at the Admiralty some time on 5 May 1915. None of the potential witnesses are still alive, and no further details are likely. Proof, either for or against, just does not exist.

9
The USS *Cyclops*

Bridgetown, Sunday, 3 March 1918. Despite the long-drawn-out European conflict, the capital of Barbados seemed hardly affected. Admittedly the price of food was much higher, whilst a general food shortage existed, but the much-vaunted U-boats and German commerce raiders had given the island a wide berth. The result was that Barbados, in terms of the wider conflict, had become something of a backwater. To keep themselves informed, therefore, residents avidly devoured a depleted stock of British and American newspapers.

On that Sunday morning, however, Barbadians were to learn of some events first hand. Anchored in the spacious roads of Carlisle Bay was the USS *Cyclops*, newly arrived from Brazil. An ungainly vessel, she was a naval collier equipped with a mass of cranes and beams which towered over her decks. Launched in 1910, the *Cyclops* was a twin-screw vessel displacing 19,600 tons. Indeed, she was the largest vessel ever to visit Barbados, and unable to enter the small harbour.

The collier's arrival off Bridgetown was totally unexpected. With no one able to explain her presence an immediate ripple of interest was created. Amongst the first to board, therefore, brought over by a custom's launch, was the US consul-general to the island, Brockhurst Livingston, together with a volunteer passport examiner and Dr J. Bridger, health officer.

Upon boarding the vessel they were greeted by the captain, George Wichman Worley. Doubtless they discovered him to be a rather strange man, made even more unusual by his refusal to give his destination – even to the US consul-general. Instead, he merely gave a reason for the ship having put into Barbados.

Apparently a miscalculation had been made, resulting in too little coal having been loaded at their last port of call. According to some of the other officers, however, this was not quite correct. According to them, one of the engines had broken down.

Whilst the ship's captain went into the more detailed needs of the ship, requesting Brockhurst Livingston to permit not only coal to be brought on board, but also money and fresh food, Dr Bridger conversed with several passengers in transit to the USA. In particular, he was to remember Lt Winkle, formerly of the USS *Pittsburgh*. Although the conversation was nothing out of the ordinary, he could not but note this particular officer's marked German accent. Indeed, he appeared more German than American.

Elsewhere, Mr E. E. H. Thorne, the volunteer passport examiner, was busily at work. He had received a request for temporary entry permits to be written out for eighteen crew members and passengers. Of those brought before him, he was distinctly surprised by a large number being of undoubted foreign origin. Several spoke with German accents, with at least three of the eighteen having unmistakable Germanic-sounding names. In a report later handed to the island's acting governor, he listed these names, which included H. Schonnof, J. M. Groff and H. Kashiwanum.

The *Cyclops* was to remain in Carlisle Bay for just over 24 hours. During this time, those who had been given entry permits were allowed ashore. They were soon to have the tiny Bridgetown community agape. Visiting downtown bars and clubs, they were full of strange stories. Some even spoke of an execution, whilst others indicated a mutiny had been attempted. Many showed a clear dislike for the captain. Some seemed to fear him, whilst one or two even suggested that he might be a German spy.

The *Cyclops*, whatever truth existed in such declarations, was an unhappy ship. For this the captain himself was mostly to blame. He was both unpredictable and thoughtless. One moment he would be full of humour, joking with crew and officers alike, the next he would be placing someone under arrest for the most trivial of disagreements. One who was particularly uncertain of Worley's character was Conrad A. Nervig. A junior officer of the watch, Nervig served in the ship for approximately two months. Taking the mid watch, he discovered that Worley was a frequent visitor to the navigation room during the dead of night. Whilst this in itself was nothing unusual, his mode of dress appeared to lack sartorial elegance. Usually clad in long woollen underwear and a derby hat, this unofficial uniform was neatly set off by a short wooden cane. Nervig was to leave the ship at Rio.

No doubt such eccentricity was for effect. Worley, from this point of view, was known throughout the fleet. Some realised him to be an incompetent officer, but most remembered him for a pre-war joke in which it was claimed that he nurtured a tame lion on board the *Cyclops*. So successfully did he carry off this piece of fiction that the Navy Department even wrote him a letter demanding that it be put ashore.

For the crew of the *Cyclops* an even greater problem revolved around the captain's standard of navigation. On numerous occasions he had jeopardised the ship, bringing her far too close into land, or threatening to destroy her on some clearly charted rock. An incident of this kind had occurred during the recent outward-bound voyage to Brazil. Sailing 43 miles past Rio Harbour, the ship's actual destination, he had allowed her to continue on a course that would have seen her grounding on dangerous shallows to the south-west. The port of Rio, apparently, had been missed during the hours of darkness.

The *Cyclops* had arrived at Rio on 28 January 1918. A few days later Worley was to demonstrate one of the reasons for which he was so hated. Ordering before him those crew members accused of one misdeed or another, he determined upon their various punishments. It was a duty which he seemed to like and which encouraged his meanest instincts. Whilst some were merely confined to ship, others received a special punishment of his own making. Drawing out a revolver, he ordered one group to remove their shoes and socks and step on to the sun-scorched metal decks. Here they remained, forced to run and move about

121

until their captain finally ordered them to sit down and be hosed with sea water.

Captain Worley's ship remained off the coast of Brazil for about a month. Here the *Cyclops* coaled a number of US warships operating in the South Atlantic before taking on a cargo of manganese ore needed by armament manufacturers back in the USA. This metallic substance, mined in Latin America, was a much sought-after mineral that was used to increase the strength of gun barrels and other similar items. It is, however, a difficult cargo to transport, having a tremendous weight. For the *Cyclops*, designed to carry coal, the manganese ore would have been loaded by volume and should also have been carefully braced to prevent shifting.

Apart from accepting a new cargo, the *Cyclops* was also given orders to take on board a number of passengers for return to the USA. Amongst this group, of course, was Lt Winkle, together with several other crew members of the battleship *Pittsburgh*. Most were being sent home for reposting, other than two petty officers, Moss Whiteside and John Morefield, together with Fireman Second Class Barney de Voe. Also former crew members of the *Pittsburgh*, they were under close arrest following an illegal drinks session in which a fellow crew member had been murdered. De Voe, who had been directly involved, had been court martialled and given a minimum of fifty years' penal servitude, whilst the two petty officers, aware of what had been going on, had been given lengthy prison sentences for failing to intervene.

Other passengers on board the *Cyclops* and returning to the USA were two marines under arrest for desertion, and a former consul-general to Brazil. The last mentioned, Alfred L. M. Gottschalk was, according to rumours circulating at the time, being relieved of his post as a result of pro-German sympathies. His Germanic-sounding name was another of those later remarked upon by Bridgetown's volunteer passport examiner.

Also under arrest, but this time a crew member of the collier, was Lt Harvey Forbes. Former executive officer, he had been placed under open arrest since the vessel's arrival in Brazil. Apparently he had clashed with the captain over that near-disaster which had occurred as a result of overshooting Rio Harbour. Forbes, a highly competent officer, had been responsible for laying the original course, but Worley had subsequently made certain alterations. These, it later transpired, were responsible for the near-tragedy, leading to a clash between Worley and his executive officer. Hard words had been passed, and Forbes was placed under open arrest.

It should also be noted that Harvey Forbes, as executive officer, would have been responsible for the taking on of new cargo. Confined to quarters, the stowing of the manganese ore was automatically overseen by a less experienced junior officer. Badly stowed, and almost certainly without any form of bracing, the cargo may well have caused problems during a later point in the voyage.

It was on 22 February that the *Cyclops* finally left the coast of Brazil, instructed to take a direct course to the USA. As such, her stop at Bridgetown, whatever the real reason, was far from planned. Indeed, it may even have been a result of one further quirk in the mind of Captain Worley.

Leaving Bridgetown late on 4 March, having received 1,500 tons of coal, together with meat, flour and vegetables, the *Cyclops* once again set course for home. On the following day she passed the British liner *Vestris*, radio signals being exchanged. The *Cyclops* on this occasion reported nothing unusual, indicating the weather to be good. This, however, was the last heard of the *Cyclops*. Like the *Waratah*, and a good many other ships that have been the centre of various maritime mysteries, she disappeared without trace.

As might be expected, a massive search was undertaken. Reported overdue on 13 March, orders were sent out for every square mile of her projected route to be searched, with each of the many islands in the areas also being visited. However, nothing further was discovered, the search being discontinued in May.

At the time numerous suggestions were given to account for

her strange loss. Considered likely was the possibility of a U-boat attack, or the ship hitting a mine. Both possibilities were ruled out, there being no enemy submarine or minelaying operations occurring anywhere within the American coastal area. Research of German naval records conducted after the war confirmed this to be the case.

Another of the possibilities considered was that the ship itself had actually been handed over to the enemy. This was certainly a view taken by the American Government. A subsequent check upon all 309 known to have been on board confirmed a sudden realisation that many had German associations. Apart from individuals referred to, this even included Captain Worley. Unbeknown to the authorities, he had actually been born in Germany, illegally entering the USA in 1878. At this time his name had the far more Germanic ring of Johann Friedrich Wichman.

In a state of near-panic, for other ships might also be threatened, the United States intelligence service placed an agent on the island of Barbados with the special brief of unearthing anything relevant to the loss of the *Cyclops*. Of even greater interest, perhaps, was that this agent had also to monitor Brockhurst Livingston. He was yet another person in the *Cyclops* story who was suspected of being pro-German. Indeed, 'Brockhurst Livingston', according to the secret service agent who entered Barbados as a member of a scientific party from Iowa University, may not even have been his real name.

A further explanation for the disappearance concerned mutiny. Already, from bar-room talk at Bridgetown, it was evident that trouble had been brewing on the *Cyclops*. As to the exact events occurring, these are as much a mystery as the cause of her final disappearance. Perhaps, indeed, such a mutiny had already occurred, with its leader having been executed. A second mutiny

The *Sportsman*, a British S-class submarine built in the Royal Dockyard at Chatham disappeared without trace in September 1952. Acquired by the French Navy, and renamed *Sybylle*, she was last seen east of Toulon during a training exercise (*RN Submarine Museum*)

124

The newly commissioned Israeli submarine *Dakar* leaves Portsmouth on her first and only voyage for the Israeli navy. A former British T-class submarine, she disappeared in the Mediterranean, bound for her new home port of Haifa (*Israeli Navy*)

may well have taken place once the *Cyclops* had left Bridgetown. Amongst those whom it has been suggested might well have been involved were some of the former crew members of the *Pittsburgh*, attempting to release their three imprisoned comrades.

Both the possibility of the *Cyclops* being handed over to the enemy, and that of her being victim of a mutiny can almost certainly be rejected. There is just so little real evidence. If handed over to the Germans, this would have been verified by documents carefully searched once the war had ended. Similarly, with mutiny. If Worley had lost control of his ship, what happened to the collier, those remaining faithful to the captain, and the mutineers themselves? If nothing else, somebody would have landed on one of the many islands in the area, but a subsequent search revealed no signs of any landing.

Because of her complete and utter disappearance, the *Cyclops* has always created considerable interest. In more recent years she has been linked with the Bermuda triangle, that area of water in the western Atlantic which has supposedly claimed so great a number of ships and aircraft. The term 'Bermuda Triangle', though, has only recently been coined. It is an area bounded by three straight lines drawn between Miami, Puerto Rico and Bermuda. Alternatively, this same area has been called the 'Devil's Triangle' and the 'Hoodoo sea'.

An unfortunate tendency now exists for any western Atlantic disappearance or mystery to be immediately thought of as occurring in the Bermuda area. Usually, however, if a ship disappears, there can be no certainty as to her exact position. The result is that many ships, some not even approaching Bermuda and its famed triangle, are claimed as victims. Nor, come to that, is there any real evidence that the seas around Bermuda are any more dangerous than certain other stretches of ocean. A strong case could be made for the dangers and mystery of the Pacific, North Atlantic and Indian oceans. In each of these extensive waters there have been strange happenings which are easily on a par with the so recently exaggerated dangers around Bermuda.

As for the *Cyclops*, there is mounting evidence to suggest that, although passing through the Bermuda Triangle, she did not succumb to its dangers – either real or imaginery. Instead. it seems likely that she reached within 70 miles of her eventual destination, the Chesapeake Bay area. This would have brought her to a point well beyond the triangle. In 1968 Dean Hawes, a naval diver, discovered a sunken ship just off the coast of Norfolk, and bearing a marked similarity to the missing *Cyclops*. Apart from being similar in size, it also had a characteristic high bridge and beams that ran the entire length of the vessel. A subsequent storm forced the dive to be abandoned, and the sunken vessel has never been relocated.

So could she have been the *Cyclops*? Certainly the vessel would have passed this point during her voyage. But what could have caused her to sink? Here more research needs to be undertaken. However, it is clear that during the second week of March, when the *Cyclops* would have been approaching Norfolk, the entire Atlantic seaboard was suffering a severe gale. Perhaps this, a combination of badly stowed cargo and her rather top-heavy design, were responsible for a tragedy so sudden that she was able neither to release lifeboats or send a radio message.

Such a theory fits those views expressed by Conrad A. Nervig. In an article written for the journal of the US Naval Institute, he draws particular attention to the cargo of manganese ore. If this had been badly stowed, perhaps confined to just two or three holds, then the *Cyclops* would have been under great stress. If during this same storm she had started to weaken, with a complete break occurring forward of the engine- and boiler-rooms, then the weight of the cargo, together with in-rushing water, would have forced both halves to sink. Nervig went on to add that the *Cyclops* had few articles that could float and it was questionable as to whether crew members could have reached these. Yet despite all this sound logic, Nervig's views are all no more than theory. In March 1918 the *Cyclops* disappeared, and until the wreck is definitely discovered, assuming she does actually lie at the bottom of the sea, nothing more can be added.

10
Fire!

Whether or not the French passenger liner *Georges Philippar* was carrying munitions for the Japanese armies about to extend their occupation of China is immaterial. What matters is that, before her maiden voyage in February 1932, a number of political activists came to believe that this was the case. As a result, the possibility of attempted sabotage exists, the intention being to prevent the vessel ever reaching her destination of Yokohama.

News that such a plot might well be in the making was first communicated to the Sûreté Général just a few days before the liner left Marseilles. At the time the threat was taken seriously, a rigorous search being undertaken. Nothing, however, was discovered. Instead, the owners of the newly commissioned liner, Messageries Maritimes, admitted that rumours of weapons being on board were not totally unfounded, the *Georges Philippar* carrying at least one quick-firing gun to be off loaded at Shanghai.

On 26 February the *Georges Philippar* duly sailed into the Mediterranean, bound for the Orient. The threat of sabotage, however, still existed. Instead of a bomb being brought on board at Marseilles, it was now suggested that an attempt would be made to destroy the vessel as she passed through the Suez Canal. For this reason the *Georges Philippar* underwent a much foreshortened stay at Port Said, where any new passengers were very carefully checked. Once again, though, nothing unusual came to light.

From now on the liner appeared to be well and truly out of danger. Certainly the rest of the voyage to Yokohama proved uneventful. Yet, on the return passage tragedy did eventually strike. Early on the morning of 16 May, whilst in the Gulf of

Aden, a fire was reported to have broken out in one of the first-class cabins. Within minutes of the report it was clear that the fire had taken quite a hold, spreading along the panelling and nearby alleyway. The master of the ship, Commandant Vicq, was immediately alerted, making his way to the scene of the fire. As it happens he was never to reach the first-class cabin in question, discovering instead that hundreds of other fires had been ignited throughout the entire ship.

Could all these fires have something to do with the threats made against the vessel whilst still at Marseilles? Certainly things were not as they ought to have been. Apart from such a large number of fires all breaking out simultaneously, it was also discovered that several chemical extinguishers had been deliberately emptied. Each fire spreading with remarkable speed, the position of many of them was often close to electrical cut-off points, so rendering useless important items of safety equipment.

Within half an hour the entire ship was ablaze. As a result, loss of life was high. Approximately forty passengers and crew were either burnt alive or drowned, most a direct result of poor organisation and limited lifeboat drill. Not surprisingly, panic also took a high toll, a number of passengers being trapped near their cabins as a result of the steel firedoors having been closed. Although Commandant Vicq later denied the charge, it is said that the screaming of helpless passengers could be heard on board even after the ship had been abandoned.

The rapid spread of the fire also prevented the radio operator sending out more than one complete SOS. Within seconds of the first distress signal being broadcast, both the cabin and wireless apparatus were ablaze. Attempts to extinguish the flames proved useless, the nearest fire extinguisher being one of those that had already been deliberately emptied.

Nevertheless, the one SOS was all that proved necessary. Six steamers were soon heading for the blazing liner, with the Russian tanker *Sovetskaia* amongst the first on the scene. Other vessels to the rescue were the *Otranto* of the Orient Line and the P&O liner *Kaisar-I-Hind*. Between them these three vessels collected over six hundred survivors, the majority being taken either to Aden or Jibouti in French Somaliland.

The *Georges Philippar*, a 21,000 ton liner, was launched at the end of 1930, total building costs amounting to £1m. Fitted with 11,600hp oil-fired engines, she had a cruising speed of 17½ knots and was considered to be particularly well equipped with a number of safety features that should have prevented her being overcome by fire. Owned and operated by the giant Messageries Maritimes company, she may or may not have been the victim of sabotage. Although an inquiry was started into her fate, no report was ever issued. Numerous interviews with both passengers and crew were conducted, but any conclusions reached were firmly withheld. Perhaps those conducting the investigation were warned off, for certainly the French Government seemed afraid of accepting sabotage as a possible explanation. This was hardly surprising; in those days leading to World War II, any such suggestion might well have led to the fall of the government or an extremist backlash from the fascist right.

The loss of three other French ships, all the result of fire and within short space of time, is one further aspect of this particular mystery. Indeed, the *Georges Philippar* herself was not the first liner so destroyed in these years. In 1928 the *Paul Lecat*, also owned by Messageries Maritimes caught fire whilst in dry-dock at Marseilles. A subsequent inquiry produced little of note, whilst the owners went ahead and commissioned a replacement. Proving something of a coincidence the new vessel, launched just two years later in the St Nazaire dockyard, was the ill-fated *Georges Philippar*. Moreover, as both ships had strong connections with Marseilles it is possible that, if sabotage was involved, then it was here that it had its origins. After all, this particular port had a noted revolutionary fervour, the town harbouring political groupings from both the fascist right and anarchist left. Perhaps one such group, determined upon the downfall of capitalism, had decided to further the cause by destroying selected prestige ships belonging to the larger French shipping companies. If this was the case, the next liner destroyed by fire was an even greater coup.

131

L'Atlantique was the second largest passenger liner serving the French marine. Of 42,000 tons and owned by the Sud-Atlantique Line, she had been specially built for the Latin-American trade. A much more impressive ship than the *Georges Philippar*, she had been completed at a total cost of £3m. First entering service in 1931, having also been launched at St Nazaire, she had a great many safety features that included both fire-proof insulation and cut-off points in her electric circuitry. However, in common with other ships of her day, much of her paint work was of a highly inflammable nature whilst furnishings, including those surrounding the staircases, bulkheads and corridors, were entirely of timber. Once a fire or series of fires started, it would spread with remarkable ease.

It was only eight months after the loss of the *Georges Philippar* that *L'Atlantique*, fortunately without any passengers on board, found herself in trouble. At 4.30am on 4 January 1933 the first indications of a problem on board was communicated to Commodore Schoofs. A fire had broken out on E deck, close to the mattress store. Fire-fighting squads were immediately detailed to the scene.

As with the previous fire that had broken out on board the *Georges Philippar*, the flames not only took a rapid hold, but appear to have broken out in several places at the same time. Again, sabotage was immediately thought a possibility. So quickly, indeed, did the fire spread that the radio operator, as with his counterpart in the Gulf of Aden, had only sufficient time to send one distress signal. Fortunately, despite it being of a very reduced strength, it was picked up by the Le Havre station, being retransmitted to all shipping in the area. The exact position of *L'Atlantique* at this time was given as 49° 30'N by 30° 17'W.

First to reach the stricken liner was the German steamer *Ruhr*, followed by the *Falmouth* and *Achilles*. All were soon hard pressed in the rescue of escaping crew members. Further off was the *Ford Castle*, a British merchantman whose captain was later to report that a red glow from the flames was visible for more than 20 miles. As his vessel approached, it was further observed that flames and sparks were shooting high into the air, rising well above a thick black cloud of smoke that had completely enveloped the passenger liner.

As for the crew of L'Atlantique, they fought valiantly to keep the blaze under control. But limited in number and having inadequate fire-fighting equipment, the task was to prove hopeless. Within two hours fire had spread throughout the length and breadth of the liner, making escape the only possible course of action. Last to leave was Commandant Schoof, driven off his own bridge by the ever encroaching flames. He, too, had struggled against overwhelming odds, severely burnt on at least two occasions. Indeed, followed around by a personal servant he had to be doused with buckets of water after his uniform had caught fire.

Once abandoned, but with fires still raging on board, the liner was an obvious danger to other shipping. Drifting towards the English coastline she was to appear off Portland on the morning of 5 January. She was still emitting smoke which occasionally prevented onlookers from seeing her, but there were other periods in which her hull was clearly visible. According to an eyewitness report that was later to appear in *The Times*, her three funnels were still standing at this time, but her foremast had gone. Her hull was 30ft out of the water, and she had a considerable list. Brought within three miles of Portland Bill, a change of wind eventually saw her taken in a more easterly direction, back towards the coast of France.

On 6 January, after a great deal of rivalry between various tug masters, she was taken in tow. Brought to Cherbourg by seven tugs, she was taken into the harbour where the last of the flames were extinguished. Masked firemen soon after descended her twisted and blackened ladders searching both for the dead and any clues as to the cause. In the engine room five charred bodies were found, but a number of crew members were to remain permanently unaccounted for. In all, seventeen were reported killed or missing. As for L'Atlantique, herself, she was to remain at Cherbourg for a number of years before being towed to the

Clyde for eventual breaking up in 1936.

The last of this series of French passenger liners to suffer the ignominy of fire was *La France*. A much older ship than those of the previous trio, she had been launched in September 1910. A four stacker, the only liner so built in France, she was designed to rival such vessels as the *Mauretania* and *Lusitania* on the highly lucrative Atlantic crossing. With decks that displayed the luxurious charms of exotic Morocco, *La France* proved particularly popular with the wealthy and influential. Proving expensive to run and eventually superseded by newer and larger vessels, she was temporarily laid up in the winter of 1932.

It was whilst in dry-dock at Le Havre that fire was to strike. As with some of those already described, the blaze was first detected in the first-class cabins on the port side. Because, on this occasion, the vessel was in port, the fire was dealt with much more effectively. Indeed, by the standards already described, the fire could be considered quite insignificant, with damage much restricted. That it occurred on 7 January 1933 with *L'Atlantique* still ablaze in the Channel is the real reason for its inclusion. Can two fires, occurring so close together, really be coincidence? The answer of course is 'yes', but it certainly stretches the imagination.

These four separate incidents of fire are interesting aspects of the French inter-war passenger liner fleet. As to whether or not sabotage was involved, it is quite impossible to say. The evidence seems fairly evenly weighted on both sides. Certainly, a number of fires seem to have been started in the same area and proceeded to spread fairly rapidly. But this could be explained by faulty wiring in the first-class cabin area, together with the inflammable nature of the furnishings. What cannot be explained quite so easily was that they should all occur in such a very short space of time. Additionally, of course, we have the evidence of the *Georges Philippar*, the ship that was not only threatened but had her chemical fire extinguishers seemingly emptied. If this was done deliberately, it is a good starting point for the sabotage theory. Yet little additional evidence has come forward, made no easier by a failure to publish the relevant inquiry reports. If it was sabotage, no responsibility has even been claimed; if it was political sabotage, this would seem essential. The other alternative is that of an individual with a particular grievance. Either way, anything further is unlikely to be uncovered. For this reason these four passenger liners must be forever connected in inexplicable mystery.

11
Two Post-War Disappearances

Sudden and unexplained disappearances at sea are not as unusual as might at first be thought. Since World War II more than 250 vessels have been lost without trace. Many are no more than small fishing boats that have capsized and taken their crews to the bottom. Others, however, are large ocean-going ships that are considered more than safe.

In 1948 two fairly large vessels, both British merchantmen, disappeared within the space of ten months. It must have proved quite a shock to the maritime world. After all, both vessels were of modern construction, steam powered and fitted with up-to-date life-saving equipment and radios. It just should not have been possible for two such vessels to disappear.

First of the vessels to hit the news headlines was the *Samkey*, a former US Liberty ship of 10,000 tons. A steel, flushed-deck vessel, she was built at Baltimore in 1943. Of all-welded construction but with riveted seams, Liberty ships such as the *Samkey* had been mass-produced throughout the war, built to replace the numerous vessels being destroyed by mines and U-boat attack. In all, 2,770 were built.

The *Samkey* herself had originally been launched as the *Carl Thusgard*, the name being changed after purchase by the New Zealand Shipping Company. It was while operating with this company that the vessel disappeared.

On 24 January 1948, the *Samkey* departed London's King George V dock on her last, ill-fated voyage. Bound for Santiago in Cuba, she had been chartered by the Ministry of Transport, but subsequently placed at the disposal of the United States Maritime Commission. She carried no cargo, having on board 1,500 tons of

Thames ballast – stones of various size mixed with sand. Her master, Captain Cremin, was not her regular master, but he had frequently sailed the Atlantic in this and other 'Sam' class Liberty ships.

At Gravesend the Thames River pilot was discharged. Later interviewed, he indicated the ship to be in excellent condition, and compared her favourably with other ships he had boarded. The New Zealand Shipping Company also had a good reputation, looking after both employees and the ships that flew their flag. Indeed, the subsequent inquiry into the loss of the *Samkey* ruled out any aspect of negligence, considering the vessel to be of a very high standard.

Yet, despite all this, something terrible obviously happened to the *Samkey*. On 31 January, whilst approaching the Azores, she transmitted her last known radio signal. Directed towards the local weather station, it was nothing more than a routine report:

Position 41° 48′N, 24°W., 12.00 GMT, Jan 31 Wind south-west 6. Weather fair. Barometer 1019 millibars, visibility 12 miles.

From then on nothing further was to be heard from the *Samkey*. Despite a considerable air and sea search, conducted both by the Portuguese air force and Ministry of Transport ships, not one clue was discovered as to her fate or that of her crew of forty-three.

The second vessel to be lost, and in rather similar circumstances, was the *Hopestar*. Somewhat smaller than the *Samkey*, being of only 5,267 gross registered tons, she had a crew of forty. Built in 1936 by Swan Hunter at their Wallsend yard, she had been surveyed by Lloyd's and carried their coveted 100 A1 classification. The *Hopestar* was of riveted construction, but had a welded inner bottom, upper and shelter deck, together with welded watertight bulkheads.

It was on Tuesday 2 November 1948 that the *Hopestar* departed from Newcastle, bound for Philadelphia. She carried no cargo, being due to take on wheat for Alexandria. Travelling in ballast, therefore, she was expected to reach the American west coast port somewhere around the middle of the month.

Taking the north of Scotland route into the Atlantic, the early part of her journey was characterised by a series of routine messages that, between them, indicated her passage. On 14 November, though, she reported storm damage: 'Heavy weather in way of top deck. Request Lloyd's and repairers on arrival'. Obviously, whatever had occurred was not considered particularly serious as the master neither called for assistance nor indicated any delay in his expected arrival date. A few hours later, at 11.30am, a final message was sent out. This time it was no more than a weather report. Wind direction was given as west-south-west and blowing at force nine. She also added her position, given as 43°N, 56° 8'W – about 150 miles south-east of Sable Island off Nova Scotia.

As with the *Samkey*, this final weather report was the last heard of the *Hopestar*. On the 22nd, then well overdue, the United States Coastguard was asked to mount a search. It proved futile. The *Hopestar* had disappeared without trace, another mystery had entered the annals of the sea.

The inquiry set up to investigate the loss of the *Samkey* sat in July 1948. It was immediately clear that a solution to her disappearance was to be no easy matter. In trying to discover a cause the inquiry would have to rely upon nothing more than conjecture and possibility. For this reason much of the attention of the court was directed to her method of ballasting, a supposed point of weakness in the 'Sam' class ships.

Unlike most ships, ballasting of a 'Sam' class Liberty ship was used, as much as anything, to reduce the vessel's top weight. In practice most cargo ships have a great deal of weight below the waterline, a feature which prevents excessive rolling. With the 'Sam' class this was quite simply not the case. Their welded construction, combined with lightweight machinery, created a vessel that not only rode high in the water but had a very fast roll. To prevent this it was necessary to reduce the overall metacentric height with ballast placed above the waterline in the 'tween-decks position. It was not, however, an altogether satisfactory arrangement, ballast located there being much more likely to shift.

Because of this, 'Sam' class ships had been subjected to a troublesome history. In 1944, for instance, the *Samevron*, a sister ship, left London with 2,025 tons of Thames ballast. During the subsequent crossing of the Atlantic, shifting had taken place and disaster was only narrowly avoided. Other 'Sam' class ships, this time sailing without ballast, had found themselves in trouble as a result of strong winds. With much of the hull above water, combined with insufficient power and limited propeller immersion, these ships had been unable to make headway.

Using the evidence of the *Samevron*, the Board of Trade enquiry found the *Samkey* to have been lost when a sudden shift of ballast in the 'tween decks had occurred. They noted that at the assumed time of her loss stormy seas had been reported and that a shift of ballast, coupled with two or three big waves, might have led to the ship being overwhelmed. Following this conclusion, an 'M' notice was issued by the Ministry of Transport to say that solid ballast, when stored in the 'tween decks, must be accompanied by shifting boards. These instructions included the rather vague statement that the boards were to be of an 'adequate' height with sufficient strength. No further guidance was given.

In reaching its conclusion, the inquiry had no real shred of evidence that the ballast on board had shifted or indeed had even endangered the ship. They placed little importance on the fact that Thames ballast has a tendency to solidify, often having to be broken out with a pick. Further, a great number of Liberty ships had used ballast in the 'tween-decks position without any shifting.

Yet the dangers cannot be denied. In September 1948 the whole matter was once again brought to the attention of the marine world. In that month the *Leicester*, a Liberty ship which sailed in ballast from Tilbury, was abandoned as a result of shifting. Unlike the *Samkey* she had been fitted with boards. On the night of 14−15 September the vessel ran into a hurricane that proved so severe that heavy seas washed the master from the navigation bridge on to the boatdeck. In spite of the boards the ballast shifted, with the *Leicester* assuming a list of approximately 40°. As a result she was abandoned.

The inquiry into the loss of the *Samkey* would not have had this information at their disposal, having made their pronouncement on 6 September. Yet the case of the *Leicester* does have a bearing on that earlier disappearance. At first sight, of course, it might appear to strengthen the court's verdict. The *Leicester* had to be abandoned but she did remain afloat. Despite appalling weather − some fairly vicious storms and a second hurricane − she was successfully towed to Bermuda. On this occasion heavy winds were responsible for driving her ashore. According to R. A. Beattie, assistant naval architect of the New Zealand Shipping Company, who subsequently examined the *Leicester*, the vessel was not in danger of sinking. Because of this, it is fair to assume that if a shift of cargo did take place on the *Samkey*, then she would have remained afloat for a sufficient length of time for the vessel to be abandoned. This, however, does not appear to have been the case.

In view of these points, it is possible to suggest that the conclusions of the inquiry were based on certain false assumptions. For one thing, the *Samkey* would probably have remained afloat, even if a fairly severe shifting of ballast had occurred, allowing the radio operator to transmit an emergency signal. In fact, he would have needed no longer than 5 seconds. Further, the lifeboat itself would have been released, this also containing, apart from emergency rations, a portable wireless. Inevitably, then, doubt must remain as to the true reason for the sudden disappearance of the *Samkey.*

Those responsible for investigating the loss of the *Hopestar* had even less to go on. The only clue concerned her penultimate radio transmission in which she reported heavy storm damage. At the time it did not appear unduly to worry the master, but complications may have arisen at a later point. This, indeed, was the factor upon which the inquiry concentrated.

First, however, a number of alternative possibilities were considered and then dismissed. Amongst them was that of a boiler explosion or of the ship being overwhelmed by high seas. Neither was considered likely. For one thing, the *Hopestar*'s boilers were in excellent condition, whilst the vessel being in ballast, her high sides presented to the sea, made overwhelming an unlikely possibility. Also considered was that of her having hit a wartime mine. With over four million having been laid, many had broken free and were still drifting. In October 1947 the *Cydonia*, a British merchantman in the Irish sea, had been victim to one of these rogue mines, and severely damaged. However, the inquiry thought this only a slight possibility, noting that most ships when struck by a mine usually go down very slowly, allowing the crew to abandon ship.

For the inquiry, an examination of the ship's past was to prove a little more profitable. In 1936, whilst still under construction, two small bunker hatches had been added to the shelter deck forward of the crew accommodation. Omitted on the plans, their subsequent inclusion had been without application to Lloyd's register. These hatches meant that the *Hopestar*, according to official estimates, was 8 per cent below the strength requirement of the then extant load-line rules. In addition, these rules were further breached in 1947 when a third main boiler was fitted into the machinery space. Replacing an original donkey boiler, the second deck was cut back without any compensation for the enlarged opening. This left the *Hopestar* 15 per cent below strength.

The inquiry, having considered the matter of reduced strength, all too easily concluded that this was the most likely cause of her loss. In his summing up, the president of the court declared that, to the best of his knowledge, the ship may simply have broken up. It was noted that bad weather coincided with her loss, helping create a split somewhere forward of the engine-room.

Yet such a conclusion must be challenged. At the time the *Hopestar* was in ballast and would have been under a much reduced strain. Certainly, for the amount of ballast carried, the remaining strength of the ship would have been more than sufficient. Further, even if the ship had broken up, one or other of the two halves would certainly have remained afloat. Without any cargo, there would be sufficient buoyancy to allow time for the crew to escape.

The court, for its part, suggested a possible scenario. According to this, the *Hopestar* disappeared sometime on the 14th. It was during this day that the master would have found it necessary to transfer water into the engine-room tanks. This manoeuvre, it was postulated, might in itself have created an excessive strain, and one made more likely by the vessel having already suffered storm damage.

Despite having arrived at this conclusion, the court seemed none too convinced that it was correct, a point confirmed when it was also stated that an outside possibility of the vessel having struck a mine also existed. In other words, despite a detailed examination, the court had no ideas as to what had really caused the loss. For this reason the *Hopestar*, even more than the *Samkey*, is a continuing mystery of the world's oceans.

Since the loss of the *Samkey* and *Hopestar*, merchant ships have continued to disappear. Fairly typical was the loss of the *Marine Sulphur Queen* in February 1963. A converted tank vessel, she was loaded with 15,260 tons of molten sulphur when she disappeared somewhere off the coast of Florida. In February 1971 it was the turn of the *Kiki* to be reported missing. A small steamer *en route* from Germany to Yugoslavia, her last message was picked up by a Dutch radio station. After that, nothing. A further case was the *El Caribe*, a Dominican-bound freighter reported missing in October 1971. At the time it was thought she might have been hijacked, but no evidence has ever been forthcoming.

More recently there was the case of the *Mark*, a 499 ton Panamanian-registered freighter, the disappearance of which has since been connected with the Penlee lifeboat disaster of 1981. The *Mark*, *en route* from Plymouth with a cargo of clay, was lost

The British submarine *Affray* was yet another submarine to disappear. Although later discovered, her partially intact hull gave little indication as to the cause of her loss (*R.N Submarine Museum*)

Spyship? *Gaul*, a deep-sea trawler which many people believe to have been involved in electronic intelligence gathering. Could this be the reason for her strange disappearance so close to the Soviet shoreline? *(Dave Sellers)*

The very last message sent by the *Gaul* was received by the *Orsino* on 8 February 1974 and indicated that the trawler had no problems *(Dave Sellers)*

sometime on 19 December, at approximately the same time as the Penlee lifeboat was engaged in its unsuccessful bid to save the crew of the *Union Star*. The subsequent loss of the lifeboat, together with eight of her crew, was heavily reported at the time. However, it also appears that other lifeboats called out to search for survivors, saw the outline of another ship which was later confirmed as being identical to the *Mark*. At the time her navigation lights were either dimmed or out. If this was the *Mark*, then it was the last seen of her, although a small amount of wreckage was later washed up close to Mount's Bay.

Mysteries such as these will remain. The disappearance of ships is no more than a fact of life. Sophisticated electronic equipment, navigational satellites and better rescue facilities will make life at sea safer, but not secure. The oceans are too powerful for this. In anger they are more than a match for the small and medium-sized freighter such as *Samkey, Hopestar* and *El Caribe*. Whether overwhelmed by freak seas or some kind of mechanical breakdown, such vessels will continue to succumb. Further, other types of vessels carry a greater and more inherent capacity for creating mysteries. These include tankers, submarines and spy ships, categories of vessel which are discussed in subsequent chapters.

12

Submarines

There was something strange and unrealistic about the German coastal submarine UB-65. Constructed during the bitter year of 1916, she was supposed to bring honour and glory to the fatherland. Instead she brought nothing but pain and suffering both to her crew and many of those who helped to build her. As far as the German navy is concerned, no vessel has ever equalled the UB-65.

Amongst the earliest who succumbed to the horrors of this U-boat were two dockyard labourers employed at the Hamburg yard of A. G. Vulcan where the UB-65 was built. Engaged in the laying of her keel, they were both struck by a huge steel girder. Badly positioned and without any warning, it came hurtling down from an overhead crane, falling on to the busy slipway. Both men were killed, one instantly; the other, pinned to the ground, underwent an hour of indescribable agony before his death.

Other victims were to follow. Amongst these were three more dockyard workmen, killed as the submarine neared completion. Inspecting the engine-room they were overcome by deadly sulphuric acid fumes emitted from one of the main batteries. These batteries, needed for powering the U-boat when submerged, were normally quite harmless. On this occasion something quite dreadful had obviously gone wrong, the men finding themselves trapped in a small enclosed space.

Eventually the UB-65, a twin-engined diesel submarine displacing 605 tons, was handed over to the navy. Doubtless it was hoped that matters would improve. Certainly there was no earthly reason for this one submarine to be any different from others of her class. Indeed, she was one of twenty-four identical vessels, all designed to undertake the same sort of work, and the only one to suffer such a multitude of problems.

In the summer of 1917 the newly commissioned submarine, operating out of the Belgian coastal port of Bruges, undertook her first seagoing voyage. Designed as nothing more than a familiarisation exercise for the crew, one or two test dives were also to be included. Edging into the North Sea, the comparatively small submarine was confronted by high winds and waves breaking over the top of her narrow bow. Visibility was severely limited. Perhaps it might have been better for the submarine to return, but the needs of war dictated otherwise.

At first there were few difficulties. The submarine seemed to perform well and easily rode the bad weather. Yet the most testing moment was the actual dive. Prior to this a petty officer had to be sent forward, instructed to check the bow planes on the outside of the vessel. According to one version he simply carried on walking, hurling himself into the sea. More likely though, he was washed overboard. Whatever the truth, another life had been claimed by the jinxed U-boat.

Matters now went from bad to worse. The test dive was attempted, but proved a truly ghastly experience. The submarine, having reached the ocean floor no more than 100ft down, simply refused to resurface. One of the tanks had developed a leak and it was a full twelve hours before the U-boat was brought under control. No one on board wished to repeat such an experience, imagining that they had been close to being permanently entombed, never to see daylight again. Matters were made no better by the dreadful atmosphere created by an emission of sulphur dioxide fumes caused by sea water entering the batteries and reacting with the sulphuric acid. As a result, many of the crew became violently ill, desperately attacking the escape hatch once the UB-65 had been brought to the surface.

Ill-luck continued to dog the submarine. Nursed into Bruges Harbour, she was suddenly the victim of a violent explosion. Unaccountably, one of the torpedo warheads had detonated, causing considerable damage to several compartments. Five crew members were killed, including the second officer.

The UB-65 now began a long period in dry-dock. Damage caused by the explosion had to be attended to, whilst repairs were needed to the leaking tank. It was not until December 1917, therefore, that the submarine was again ready for active service. This time, however, there was to be a further twist to the story. For as crew members returned, some having been given a short period of leave, an ordinary seaman rushed into the wardroom. Appearing ashen-faced, he announced to the astonished captain that both he and another crew member had witnessed the former second officer, so recently killed, walking up the gangway. The UB-65 was now haunted!

Throughout the first few months of 1918 several crew members were to report seeing the second officer. Frequently he was to be found, arms folded, either on the conning tower or on the foredeck. Because of this, many now refused to serve on board, with a great number seeking a transfer. Others merely deserted. Life at this time is best described by one of the petty officers who had served on board since the vessel had been first commissioned:

> UB-65 never was a 'happy' ship, though we were always fortunate in our officers. There was something in the atmosphere on board which made one uneasy. Perhaps, knowing her evil history, we imagined things, but I am convinced myself that she was haunted. One night at sea I saw an officer standing on deck. He was not one of us. I caught only a glimpse of him, but a shipmate who was nearer swore that he recognised our former second officer, who had been killed long before by a torpedo explosion. On other nights, while lying on my bunk, I saw a strange officer walk through the ship. He always went in the forward torpedo room but never came out again. Several of the bluejackets saw the ghost quite often, but others were unable to see it, even when it was pointed out to them standing only a few feet away.

Most now considered the UB-65 to be doomed. Certainly none of the crew expected to survive the war, and for one, a torpedo gunner, it all became too much. During the month of May, with the U-boat operating in the Bay of Biscay, he suddenly ran the entire length of the ship screaming unintelligibly. It later transpired that he had actually rubbed shoulders with the former second officer, and was only calmed down by a dose of morphia. The following morning he was much calmer, being allowed on deck in the charge of a rating. In the event this proved fatal. The gunner's madness seized him once again and he threw himself over the side. His body was never recovered. Two days later, whilst helping mount the single gun forward of the conning tower, another crew member, Richard Meyer, was swept overboard.

On 10 July 1918 the UB-65 was to meet her fate. But even this was no straightforward affair. That morning, whilst lying off Cape Clear in the eastern Atlantic, she was spotted by the American submarine AL2. The latter, travelling at periscope depth, was gently manoeuvred into position prior to unleashing a pair of bow torpedoes. Before this could be accomplished the German U-boat was suddenly enveloped in a mass of smoke. The UB-65 had exploded, the reason for which remains a mystery. The last that the American commander saw of her was a German officer, arms folded, standing on the conning tower. Was this the second officer finally put to rest?

It is the submarine more than any other seagoing vessel that is the most likely creator of sea mysteries. Travelling beneath the ocean's surface there is much that can go wrong, with only the immediate crew aware of its full consequence. Thus a submarine may disappear because of a faulty depth gauge leading the vessel to sink beneath its maximum design depth. Alternatively, poor navigation may result in the vessel hitting an underwater object or becoming trapped. In either case debris may be sparse, with the outside world quite unaware of the boat's exact location.

Undoubtedly the greatest danger is that of being rammed by a surface vessel. Travelling underwater, sometimes no more than a few feet below the surface, the submarine is an easy victim for any unwary ship that enters the same stretch of water. Furthermore, modern oil tankers, especially the Ultra Large Crude Carriers (ULCC), have a maximum draft in excess of 80ft. Their sheer size and power may also mean that they are quite oblivious to any collision, which would send an unfortunate submarine instantly to a watery grave.

Perhaps one of the earliest of British submarine mysteries resulted from this very cause. On 12 November 1925, the M-1, a monitor submarine with 12in external guns, failed to return from a diving exercise in the English Channel. The Admiralty announced her loss later that same evening:

> During exercises early this morning submarine M-1 was seen to dive in a position about 15 miles south of Start Point. She has not been seen since. Every effort is being made to locate her and establish communication.

Despite an extensive search lasting well into the second week of December, nothing was ever found of the missing submarine or her crew of sixty-eight.

At first the loss was considered to be a result of the submarine having dived too steeply, striking the bottom and turning turtle. The M-class submarines, of which only three were built, were notoriously fast divers, the weight of the large guns making them difficult to control. Indeed, what normally happened was that the submarine would be allowed to dive at an inordinate speed, with correction taking place upon full immersion.

As a solution to the loss of the M-1, this particular theory was rapidly discarded. Instead, some ten days later, a report was received that a Swedish cargo vessel, the *Vidar*, whilst close to the submarine's last known position, had hit some sort of underwater object. The incident had not been reported earlier, as the captain had been late in hearing of the loss of the submarine. At the time high seas had been running, with the *Vidar*, a vessel that normally draw 18ft 8in, plunging deeply. Dry-docked on 25 November, the hull of the *Vidar* was examined, revealing that in addition to certain dents, there were grey-green paintmarks identical to that of the M-1, whose upper decks had been recently painted.

A further submarine thought to have been struck by a cargo vessel was the *Ondine* of the French navy. Undertaking her first 'shakedown' cruise during October 1928, it seems likely that she was run down by the Greek freighter *Ekaterina Goulandris* sometime during the night of 4 October. Unlike the M-1, the *Ondine* would have been on the surface but providing a low, ill-lit silhouette which the crew of the *Ekaterina Goulandris* may not have seen. Suspicion was directed towards the Greek freighter when she later reported hitting 'wreckage' at a point where she would have intersected the *Ondine*, then on a direct course from Cherbourg.

Not all submarine mysteries are as easy to solve. Many of these vessels simply disappear without leaving any clues whatsoever. Into this category fall two French submarines, the *2326* and the *Sybylle*. Both were new to the French navy, but had seen previous service. The *2326* was a former German U-boat, surrendered to the Royal Navy and handed over to the French in February 1946. Indeed, she was still undergoing trials when she disappeared without trace on 6 December of that same year. Involved in deep-sea diving tests, she was last reported as being not too distant from Toulon, just south of Cap Cepot. No wreckage was ever found, though it was thought possible that she had hit a wartime mine.

The *Sybylle*, taken over from the Royal Navy in 1951, was a former S-class submarine, the *Sportsman*, built at Chatham in 1942. Whilst undergoing a training exercise in the Mediterranean and in company with her escort *Le Touareg*, she disappeared east of Toulon on 24 September 1952. No wreckage was ever found. It has since been assumed that the crew, unfamiliar with the design of British submarines, made some kind of fundamental error that might well have taken her well below her safe depth. Alternatively she might have become damaged upon hitting the ocean floor.

Nowadays the possibility of a submarine completely disappearing has been much reduced. The development of deep-sea rescue units together with oceanographic research ships fitted with various sensor devices and cameras means that any missing submarine has a much greater chance of being rediscovered. The US Navy, in particular, has a large number of such vessels, and had cause to use them following the loss of both the *Thresher* and *Scorpion.* In neither case, however, was it possible to raise the hull, both submarines being too deep. Instead, photographs were taken for the purpose of trying to discover the cause of the losses.

It was on 10 April 1963 that the *Thresher*, with 130 men, was announced as 'overdue and presumed missing'. Earlier that day she had been undergoing deep-diving tests, remaining in permanent contact with her escort vessel, *Skylark.* At 09.00hrs (EST), whilst 200 miles east of Boston, she undertook the first of a series of dives. According to Lt Watson, radio operator on board the *Skylark*, giving evidence at a subsequent inquiry, the *Thresher* sent an urgent message indicating that she was having to blow out air in order to regain the surface. No panic was discernible. Her next message was garbled. According to Lt Watson:

> We heard sounds that are familiar to me, from having seen ships blown up by torpedo in World War Two: the sound of a ship breaking up, like a compartment collapsing.

Unlike some of the other submarines described, the exact area of her disappearance was immediately narrowed to a few thousand square yards. But this did not really make the task particularly easy, as the depth of water was approximately 8,400ft. Immediate efforts to locate the submarine proved futile, with the major search effort having to await the arrival of more specialised equipment, such as the *Trieste*, a bathyscaphe designed for such depths.

The *Thresher* was eventually located at the end of May. Having imploded as a result of falling to such a depth, she was nothing more than a mass of twisted steel debris which offered little in the way of clues. Floating in the Atlantic there was also discovered a fragment of plastic shielding identified as coming from the *Thresher.* This showed signs of having been hit by a sheet of flame. With nothing else to go on, the enquiry also examined the history of the *Thresher*, discovering that she had been subjected to a number of mechanical difficulties in the past.

Only two weeks prior to her destruction a fast cruise test had been cancelled because of problems with planes, angle indicators and air systems. Because of all this, the inquiry suggested that some similar malfunction had occurred, leading to other and more serious complications.

Lost in 1968 was the second of the two US submarines referred to, the *Scorpion*. Returning to her home base from the Mediterranean, she made a routine radio transmission on 21 May, giving a position south-west of the Azores. This was to be the last heard of the submarine and her crew of ninety-nine. An extensive search was inaugurated, but it was not until October that the *Mizar*, an oceanographic research ship, eventually discovered the wrecked hull. Photographs showed the superstructure to be intact, but lying on its side and more than 100ft from the bow. The eventual inquiry on this occasion felt unable or unwilling to indicate a cause, although it was admitted that she was 27 miles off course due to involvement in some kind of secret mission.

Most intriguing of modern-day mysteries concerns the French diesel-powered submarine *Minerve*. Disappearing on 27 January 1968, her wreckage has still to be discovered. The *Minerve*, one of the highly successful 'Daphne' class submarines, was launched at Nantes in 1961, prior to entering service three years later. Considered to be of particularly sound design, a number of the world's navies have since based their own submarine-building programmes upon this particular class.

On the morning that the *Minerve* disappeared, she had been due to undertake special detection exercises some 20 miles off Toulon. Working in company with a Breguet Atlantic of the naval air service, she was first to help calibrate the aeroplane's radar before playing a rather sophisticated game of 'cat and mouse'. The Atlantic, therefore, duly arrived over the exercise area at a little after 7.00am, but due to poor weather had difficulty in maintaining radio contact with the submarine. For this reason it was decided to cancel the exercise, the Atlantic being ordered to return to its airfield at Nimes-Canon. Lt de Vaisseau Quinnec, pilot of the aircraft, later reported that radio contact with the submarine was abruptly lost at 7.55am. At the time it was not considered unusual, it being assumed that the *Minerve* had submerged in order to avoid the rapidly deteriorating weather.

Continued lack of radio contact, and the *Minerve*'s failure to enter Toulon Harbour the following morning, alerted the authorities to the likelihood of something having gone wrong. An immediate search was instituted, but despite large numbers of participating ships, aircraft and helicopters, nothing definite was to be found. The only possible exception was an oilslick south-west of Cape Sicie and close to the training area. If this had been released from the *Minerve*, it strongly suggested that she was lying on the ocean floor some 6,500ft below.

The suggested reasons for the loss are countless. Most recognise that some sort of accident must have taken place, the *Minerve* being consequently dragged well below her design depth of between 1,–2,000ft. Eventually the hull would have come under such immense pressure that implosion was all but certain. Because of the lack of more definite evidence early ideas tended to resolve around those factors most commonly associated with other submarine losses: collision, technical failure or the striking of a mine.

As already indicated, the single most frequent cause for submarines being lost is that of collision with surface ships. The *Minerve*, possibly at periscope depth, but certainly hidden by storm-tossed waves, could easily have been run down. At the time that detection exercises with the Breguet Atlantic were to have taken place, the pilot reported the existence of two merchantmen, although not within the immediate area of the submarine. The pilot went on to admit that other vessels, undetected by the aeroplane's radar due to poor weather, might have been appreciably nearer.

The striking of a mine, although not very likely, cannot be overruled. In spite of careful dredging, wartime mines, even to this day, are still known to exist in the area. For this reason submarines, when entering certain sectors, are not allowed to dive within 100ft of the ocean floor.

The possibility of a technical fault was the main aspect upon which a later commission of inquiry concentrated itself. Although it came up with no particular conclusions, reference was made to the possible failure of electrical circuits, torpedo tubes or batteries. Lack of any wreckage prevented further investigation.

Another suggestion connects the loss of the *Minerve* with an equally mysterious disappearance, that of the Israeli submarine *Dakar*. Both vessels were operating in the Mediterranean at approximately the same time, making final contact with the outside world within hours of one another. As with the *Minerve*, no clues exist for the sudden and unexplained loss of the *Dakar*.

The Israeli submarine, recently purchased from the Royal Navy, was in the process of being ferried from Portsmouth to her new base of Haifa. Although launched as the *Totem* in 1943, the newly named *Dakar* had undergone an extensive refit that should have seen her undertaking a good many more years of active service. According to the Israeli authorities, she gave her last position report at midday on 26 January, being at that time 100 miles off Cyprus. After that she failed to make further contact. An extensive air and sea search, including the involvement of three RAF Shackletons, failed to reveal any signs of wreckage.

Of course, it must be admitted as strange that two submarines with only 1,500 miles of water between them should both disappear within a twenty-four-hour period. It is a fact that has not gone unnoticed by other writers, consideration often being given to strange and unnatural forces. Alternatively, some kind of double sabotage has also been put forward, a point which the Israelis certainly rule out. As for the French, they appear to have had no particular enemies at that time. Another plausible theory accounting for both losses is that of the two submarines being engaged in a planned rendezvous for the exchange of missiles. At the time Israel was desperately short of such weapons, with the French able to supply most of their needs. Of course, the French government would not wish such a transaction to be made public because of their own delicate relationships with various Arab states. This version of the double loss makes the further assumption that during the actual exchange something went desperately wrong, resulting in the explosion of a warhead. The idea is strongly undermined by the lack of reported wreckage in any part of the Mediterranean during the following week.

Strange and uncertain vessels, submarines deserve a book to themselves; the few mentioned here are merely a representative sample of hundreds of other unaccountable stories that beg inclusion. Reference could certainly have been made to numerous wartime disappearances or, perhaps, the strange fate of the *Affray*, a British submarine that disappeared in the Channel during April 1951. Although later discovered partially intact, no one could indicate a reason for her loss. Alternatively, the frequent spying and espionage missions of both Soviet and American submarines, together with German U-boats during World War II, could provide a host of even greater mysteries. This becomes clear if the loss of the *Scorpion* is remembered. After all, what was that secret mission that took her 27 miles off course? What is there southwest of the Azores that so interested the Americans at that time? Doubtless these questions might be answered in the future, but at this precise moment they are further unknowns of the submarine world.

13
The Veronica Mutiny

An air of mystery has always surrounded events taking place on board the three-masted barque *Veronica* in December 1902. For reasons unknown, several crew members organised and carried out one of the most bloody and pointless mutinies ever to have been witnessed on the high seas. In all, seven men were killed as a result, each being shot or bludgeoned to death without compassion. For those involved there was nothing to gain other than the knowledge that they would be forever on the run from justice, fugitives from an act that could be discovered at any time in their lives.

The *Veronica*, although a British ship and registered in Liverpool, was one of those small coastal traders that spent much of her working life in foreign waters. Captained by Alexander Shaw, the vessel rarely visited her homeland. Instead, she was a familiar site along the South and Central American coastline, engaged in the movement of numerous general cargoes.

From this point of view, the year 1902 was nothing unusual. A contract had been signed, and the *Veronica* was engaged in the carriage of timber between Ship Island in the Gulf of Mexico and the port of Montevideo, Uruguay. The passage there and back, made under sail, took just over four months, the *Veronica* returning to Ship Island in August. After a short period in quarantine, she began loading a new cargo in September.

Amongst the earliest problems confronting Captain Shaw was the need for a new crew. The lengthy loading period of nearly a month meant that most of those hired for the previous voyage had sought work elsewhere, only three choosing to stay with the *Veronica*. Those remaining, therefore, were Moses Thomas, a negro cook, and two ordinary hands, Otto Monsson and Harry Flohr who were both of German nationality.

For the rest of his crew, Alexander Shaw had to venture on to Ship Island, a tough port that seems to have collected the very dregs of the sea. But this did not unduly worry the captain of the *Veronica*. He knew the port well, and had a great deal of experience in handling difficult men. Indeed, Shaw himself was noted for his strong discipline, but was in no way cruel. Not, therefore, the most popular of masters, he was, however, respected.

As in all such cases, the quest for a replacement crew began with an approach to certain self-assigned boarding masters. For a fee, usually thirty dollars a head, such individuals would supply some of those required hands. First to be contracted was Fred Abrahamson, a tough and embittered character who had once sailed with Shaw. Employed since the previous year in the supplying of crews, Abrahamson was none too worried as to how he earnt his thirty dollars. Rumour had it, for instance, that he had been responsible for 'shanghaing' a sailmaker from a certain Norwegian barque, placing him on board an American schooner. As likely as not, the rumour was true, for Abrahamson was desperate to get away from Ship Island since the authorities were about to bring him to justice. The result was that this Swedish-born 'no good' also agreed to be one of those who should sign on with the *Veronica*. Despite his reputation, however, agreed by many as the worst of a bad lot, Abrahamson was not one of those who mutinied, staying loyal to Alexander Shaw.

The real troublemakers were Gustav Rau and Willem Smith, two of the hands that Abrahamson brought with him. Rau, of German nationality, was later to lead the mutiny having brought a gun on board the *Veronica*. Even before the vessel sailed, he showed himself true to the traditions of such a wayward port as Ship Island, approaching fellow German Harry Flohr in an attempt to persuade him to desert. The plan was that the two of them should board one of the loading craft and then take a fee for joining another ship. Flohr, an eighteen-year-old youth and later to succumb to the threats of Gustav Rau, turned the suggestion down, telling Rau that he would inform the captain.

That neither Rau nor Smith were using their real names was a further indication that they were characters to be avoided. It is possible that Rau, whose real name was August Mailahn, was a deserter from the German navy, having been in the Imperial service up to 1901. Perhaps this was the reason he had changed his name, although equally he might have had something else to hide. Willem Smith on the other hand, a Dutchman who had changed his name from Dirk Herlaar, had originally been dismissed from one German ship for theft, then joining the *Linse* which he had recently deserted at Ship Island.

Other crew members recruited by Shaw were to play a much less prominent part in forthcoming events. First amongst these was Alexander MacLeod, the chief mate, and Pat Dorran, an Irishman whom Shaw appointed as first mate. Additionally there were two more Swedes, Gus Johanssen and Julius Parssons, together with Alec Bravo, referred to as a Lascar and a native of India. In each case their primary role was that of victim, being marked men for a seemingly blood-crazed Gustav Rau.

Sailing on 11 October, the first incident to occur on board the *Veronica* that might have had some bearing on the future mutiny was when Willem Smith was struck by Pat Dorran. This took place just three days after leaving Ship Island and as a result of Smith refusing to haul the top gallant and royal brace. It is possible that Smith now nurtured a grudge that was eventually to be shared by Rau and, to a lesser extent, Otto Monsson.

That both Smith and Rau had now developed a close friendship was obvious. Additionally, Monsson had known Rau before they had joined the *Veronica*, and the three formed a small group that kept itself from the rest of the crew. Clearly led by Rau, they seemed determined that the young Harry Flohr should also join them, probably because of his German nationality. Flohr, for his part, preferred to avoid his fellow countrymen, finding Gustav Rau a particularly difficult man to get on with. The result was that the two had little mutual contact for about a month.

159

It was just a few days before the mutiny itself that Flohr was once again approached. This time it was by both Monsson and Rau, the two of them informing Flohr that their lives were in danger. According to Rau a plot was being organized by the chief mate. Informing Flohr of the details, he went on to say, 'We will soon be thrown overboard. I heard the chief mate and the second mate talking and that they were going to throw both you and Monsson overboard'.

Rau had obviously given much thought to what was nothing but a highly contrived fairy tale. It could certainly not have had any basis of truth, and Flohr must have realized this. But Rau, standing there on the forecastle of the *Veronica*, continued, 'We want to kill them and throw them overboard before they kill us. Monsson and Smith are already agreed and they want you to help as well.' Flohr, who had appreciably paled at such a suggestion, said he could not: 'I can hardly see a pig killed. How can I see a man?'

But nevertheless Rau proved very persuasive. He pointed out that he had brought a gun on board and that there were plenty of belaying pins* lying around. Besides which, if he did not agree to help, so Rau threatened, then Flohr would go the same way as the others. The eighteen year old was gradually reduced to tears and, not surprisingly, eventually agreed.

The mutiny took place three days later, on Sunday 7 December. It was clearly Rau who was the originator of the affair, telling both Smith and the two other Germans exactly what he expected of them. The first move was to be against the mate, Pat Dorran. Flohr was simply told, 'Just walk up to him and push a knife into his throat'.

In the end, however, it was Rau who carried out the task. Sometime around 3.00am he approached the first mate who was at that time standing watch on the forecastle deck. Engaging him in conversation, Rau asked him if he could see the North Star. Without waiting for a reply he quickly passed behind the mate

*Belaying pin. An iron or wooden bar used to fasten the running rigging of a sailing ship. Readily available, they were stored inside the bulwarks or at the base of each mast.

and struck him with an iron belaying pin. Dorran immediately
fell to the deck whereupon he was struck once more. Still not
dead, he was pulled into one of the port lockers, and Flohr was
ordered to guard him. Later, the mate showed signs of life so he
was simply thrown overboard – a fate yet to be shared by a good
many others.

The mutineers, now committed to their task, acted in a rapid
and certain manner. Fellow crew members were soon being
attacked thick and fast. Alexander MacLeod, searching for the
first mate, proved an easy target. Wandering about the foredeck,
he was struck across the back of the neck and his lifeless body
pushed into the sea. The next target was Gus Johanssen, the man
at the wheel. Thanks to Harry Flohr his life was to be spared just
a little longer than it might have been. The young German,
sickened at the very idea of killing someone, took, not an iron
belaying pin but one of the much lighter wooden ones. Striking
Johanssen across the back of the head there was insufficient force
to cause real injury, leaving the Swede stunned but mobile.
Abandoning the wheel he ran to the forecastle and was to plead
successfully for his life, throwing in his lot with the mutineers.

Also to be killed at this stage was Julius Parssons who, upon
hearing the noise above, tried to crawl out of his cabin porthole.
As he did so he was struck over the head, his limp body being
thrown over the side of the ship. The attacker on this, as on many
subsequent occasions, was Gustav Rau.

Now it was the turn of Alexander Shaw, a man who had rapidly
lost all authority. Having come on deck he was, due to severe
deafness, quite oblivious to events going on around him. This was
not to make any difference, however. Rau, having spotted him,
hurled an iron belaying pin that caught Shaw on the chest.
Almost certainly breaking a few rib bones, the captain just
managed to make the bottom of the stairs and the comparative
safety of the navigation room.

Last to be attacked that night was Fred Abrahamson. He was
aroused by a series of shots that had been fired in the general
direction of the captain as he had fallen down the stairs. Emerging

on deck, Abrahamson was also fired upon, running into the saloon crying, 'Oh Lord Captain, I'm shot'.

All this time Moses Thomas, the only loyal crew member to survive the mutiny, was trapped in his cabin afraid to come out. Also woken by a number of pistol shots, he heard Rau calling out, 'I have killed the captain, the chief officer and the second officer, nobody left but the cook'. Now addressing his remarks towards Thomas, he continued to shout, 'Come out you black son of a bitch, come out'. The cook wisely decided to secure his room, carefully bracing the door.

It was not until morning, when the general noise had died down, that he felt safe to investigate the situation. Entering the saloon he was immediately confronted by Rau, pistol in hand, who shouted, 'Come up you son of a bitch, come up'. As he walked forward, Smith interposed and said, 'Don't kill the poor cook, he hasn't done anything, it's a pity to kill the man'. Brought back, perhaps, to a form of temporary sanity, Rau agreed. Instead of meeting his death, Moses Thomas was ordered to the galley where he was to make coffee for all of them; presumably in the cook's absence, the others had dwelt on his fate.

Apart from Thomas, the mutineers had both Fred Abrahamson and the captain still to deal with. Both had now taken refuge in the navigation room and were refusing to leave this area of comparative safety. At first they were simply left alone, kept there in a wounded condition and without sustenance. But eventually, so it was decided, the situation could not be allowed to continue, especially as Rau needed charts and a sextant for steering. Opening a skylight this ruthless killer called down for those things he needed. The second mate, Abrahamson, replied in a weakened voice that the captain was far too ill. Rau, however, persisted and the captain seems to have crawled out and spoken. He made a piteous appeal in which he asked, 'What have I done that I should be treated like this? We never knew that anything wrong was going on on board the ship. Why did you not tell me if anything was going wrong? I have a wife and children.

Cannot you not spare my life? Give me some water at any rate.'

The captain and Abrahamson were left a few more days until it was decided that it was no longer safe to keep them alive. The two were therefore ordered out, being told that their lives would be spared. As Abrahamson put his head round the door he saw that the mutineers were fully armed and obviously intent upon his murder. Making a dash for it, he reached the starboard side of the ship, fired upon by Smith who wounded him in the shoulder. Throwing himself over the side he swam for all he was worth. His escape could not be permitted, Rau giving the order ' 'Bout ship. We cannot sail on and leave him alive, so he must be killed before we leave him out of sight − 'bout ship.' Soon, therefore, under a hail of bullets, the body of the second mate was seen to slip below the surface. Another victim had been claimed.

Then it was the turn of the captain. Ordered out of the navigation room he failed to appear. Instead Alec Bravo, whose life had been spared on the night of the mutiny, was sent in with an axe to drive the captain out. The dying man made his way to the stairs. For him there was to be no last minute dash. He was both too old and too weak. Instead, he slowly mounted each step, aware that his last moments had arrived. Reaching the top, a pistol was placed at his head; Rau, holding the weapon, pulled the trigger. Falling backwards, Alexander Shaw collapsed into the navigation room.

By now only seven of the original crew were still alive. Apart from the mutineers, there was Moses Thomas, Gus Johanssen and Alec Bravo. Whilst no reason was given for saving some and killing others, it is clear that Rau, Smith and Monsson saw the need for a few additional crew members to sail the boat. Moses Thomas, for instance, a useful man in the galley but certainly no seaman, was expected both to take a turn at the wheel and also the pumps.

It is unlikely that those surviving loyal crew members expected to survive indefinitely. Each had witnessed the extremes of cruelty to which Rau had sunk, and they themselves must have felt death to be very close. To encourage continued co-operation, however, each crew member was told to learn a version of events that would prevent the mutineers being brought to justice. Instead of Rau being responsible for the deaths of so many, it was to be said that a fire had occurred, as a result of which the *Veronica* had to be abandoned. Two life-boats had been launched, with the captain and part of the crew in one, and they in the other. Since the outbreak of the fire, so it was to be said, nothing had been seen of the captain's life-boat, nor anything else of those particular crew members.

Failure to learn the full details of the story, including the exact position of the fire and sequence of events, ultimately led to the deaths fo Gus Johanssen and Alec Bravo. Neither could recite details given, and their elimination was considered the only safe solution. First to be killed in this new wave of murders was Johanssen, shot by Smith in the stomach. This, however, proved far from fatal, the wound later being dressed by Moses Thomas. On the following day Smith made a further attempt, this time shooting Johanssen in the head.

The final victim of the *Veronica* mutiny was Alec Bravo. Engaged in work upon the rigging, he was perched up on one of the masts when Gustav Rau took a shot at him. Possibly resulting in instant death, Bravo's body fell directly into the sea. According to Thomas, who witnessed the event, his life was also at risk, a pistol being turned on him as well. Miraculously, though, the gun jammed, allowing the cook to take refuge in the forecastle. Here he managed to convince the various mutineers of his usefulness, promising that he would never give them away.

Moses Thomas' survival is, in fact, a further mystery to the whole story. Having no part in the mutiny and therefore nothing to hide, he was always at liberty to break his promise of silence which, after all, had only been extracted under duress. It must therefore be suggested that the mutineers took a liking to him or, quite possibly, felt that no one would ever believe such an incredible sequence of events. After all, given the racial bias of the times, the cook was a negro and it would be his word against four whites.

The deaths of Johanssen and Bravo created an immediate problem, since there were now insufficient hands to sail the *Veronica* and plans had to be made to abandon her. Orders were given for a lifeboat to be newly caulked and a mast and sail added. This work was carried out from 16 December onwards and, once completed, the boat was fully provisioned.

On Saturday 20 December the boat was duly hoisted over the side, with Rau supervising the agreed destruction of the *Veronica*. Timber was chopped up and piled in the after cabin whilst items of blood-stained clothing, soaked in paraffin, were placed on top. Just before their departure, and to add a potential note of realism, the second lifeboat was also launched in the hope that if it was picked up by another vessel it would strengthen the belief that the crew had escaped in two boats. Lowered into the water, an attempt to capsize the second lifeboat failed, so the mutineers had to leave her to float upright. After this the *Veronica* was set alight and abandoned.

Sailing the lifeboat on a south-easterly course, land was eventually sighted on Christmas Day. Estimated as part of the north-east coast of Brazil, Rau gave orders for all remaining provisions to be thrown overboard together with navigation equipment. Moving closer to the shoreline, they were eventually to land on the uninhabited island of Cajueira which lies at the mouth of the Parnaíba River. For their purposes it was a rather unfortunate land fall as the island belonged to the Liverpool trading company of Hugh Evans. Used for purposes of warehousing it was a regular port of call, with a company ship due within a couple of days.

On 28 December the five remaining crew members of the *Veronica* were taken on board the Liverpool-registered *Brunswick*. Rau immediately informed the ship's master, George Brown, of their circumstances, repeating that carefully rehearsed account that had been worked out some weeks earlier. As for the master of the *Brunswick*, he was to make the following entry into his log:

I have this day taken on board five members of the crew of the barque *Veronica* of St. John's, New Brunswick, which vessel was burnt at sea on the 20th December 02, they having arrived at the island of Cajueira Barra de Tutoia Coast of Brazil on the 25th December 02 in a state of complete destitution being only partially clothed, and having been five days in the boat. Their provisions when they left the ship consisted of one small barrel of water, and eleven biscuits. There being no Consul at this place and no one to help them or give them food, as the island is only inhabited by native labourers during the stay of our vessel there, I have taken them on board in order to hand them over to their Consul at Lisbon to which port we are bound. I have examined several of them and all agree that the barque *Veronica* of St. John's N.B., left Ship Island, USA, on 11th October 02 bound to Monte Video with a cargo of lumber. Alexander Shaw, Master. Crew 12 hands . . .

On the 20th December fire was discovered on board and the vessel soon became hopelessly on fire, and the crew abandoned the ship. The second mate and four men left in one boat and the captain (and remaining crew) in the other. The boats separated and nothing has been heard of the captain's boat since to their knowledge or ours.

On the voyage to Lisbon the story of the *Veronica* was obviously discussed by the crew of the *Brunswick*. Clearly they were not satisfied with everything as it had been explained. For instance, Smith had apparently stated, 'Oh, we had to leave the *Veronica* in such a hurry that we could not even find time to get our caps. That is why none of us have caps.' Then came the comment from some of the sailors of the *Brunswick*, 'Well, that is an odd thing, because you found time to bring with you, in a bag, a new suit of clothes and a new pair of brown boots'. On another occasion the matter of mixed nationalities cropped up, and someone on board the Brunswick said to Smith, 'It is very strange that so many of the survivors should be German'. Smith's answer was, 'Oh not at all, not at all, because we were all on the same watch'.

The mutineers, of course, now had little control over Moses Thomas. Upon arriving on board the *Brunswick* he had asked if he could be quartered away from the other *Veronica* crew members, preferring to berth with the *Brunswick*'s own cook.

166

Avoiding any contact with Rau, he eventually decided that he should inform Captain Brown of the full truth. On 21 January 1903, after reaching Lisbon, the following entry was made into the log book of the *Brunswick*:

> Moses Thomas of the barque *Veronica* of St. John's New Brunswick and one of the members of the ship-wrecked crew on board this vessel did on the 12th day of January 1903 make a statement to me privately that the other four men led by Gustav Rau did before the barque was burnt kill the captain and mate and also attempt to kill him. This statement I have communicated to H.M.B. Consul at Lisbon who ordered me to make this entry in the Official Log and take the men to Liverpool and hand them to the authorities.

Upon her arrival at Liverpool the mutineers were consequently taken away by the police and subsequently tried at the Liverpool Spring Assizes of May 1903. Giving evidence for the prosecution were both Harry Flohr, who had turned King's evidence, and Moses Thomas. For the most part their stories tallied and has been used in this account to describe the mutiny. As for Rau, Smith and Monsson, their accounts differed widely, although an attempt was made to place the blame upon the shoulders of Moses Thomas. Amongst other things it was suggested that it was he who had originaly supplied the information about the mate's plan to throw two of the Germans overboard. It was also said, following the fight between officers and men on 7 December, that the cook had taken over the ship, imprisoning both the captain and second mate. Obviously, the jury found it difficult to accept such a version, especially as it was Thomas who had indicated that the *Veronica* had not been destroyed accidentally.

The trial itself lasted exactly three days. At 9.00pm on 15 May the jury, having retired for a mere fifteen minutes, passed a unanimous verdict of guilty. The judge, in complete agreement, sentenced all three to death, although Monsson later had his sentence commuted to penal servitude for life. Rau and Smith, therefore, were hanged at Walton Prison on 2 June, the former still proclaiming innocence.

Yet the mystery of why the mutiny took place still remains.

167

Little or no indication of this was produced in the trial, whilst nothing was later added by any of those involved. It was a strange affair in which the mutineers must surely have had some hidden reason for their deeds. After all, the murder of seven fellow crew members can hardly have been without some motive. A simple grievance against Pat Dorran could certainly not have led to a wholesale massacre. Yet this is what it outwardly appeared. Even more surprising than the apparent lack of motive was the failure to kill Moses Thomas. Had he been included amongst those who had been murdered, it is unlikely that this chapter could ever have been written. The crew of the *Brunswick* may have had their suspicions, but they had no proof. Moreover, it seems that they accepted most of what they were told. The truth, as related by the black cook changed everything, and meant that justice could take its course.

14
Spyship?

The *Gaul*, a British deep-sea trawler of 1,106 tons and once the pride of Hull, could well have been a spyship. Amongst all her electronic gadgetry which included radar scanners and sonar, there might also have been included, but carefully hidden away, intelligence-gathering equipment of a highly sophisticated nature. If this was the case, and the evidence is strong, then it might well explain her strange disappearance in February 1974. Trawling some 70 miles off North Cape, and only a short distance from the Arctic coastline of the Soviet Union, she would also have had on board naval officers responsible for the operation of intercept receivers designed for the monitoring of Soviet shipping movements.

For its part, the Royal Navy has always denied using trawlers for such operations, but such denials must not always be taken at face value. During the 1950s, when it was permissible for Hull trawlers to work within 3 miles of the Soviet coastline, British naval officers were frequently taken on board for the purpose of observing Soviet warships at sea. Moreover, following upon enquiries into the loss of the *Gaul*, it was further admitted that some trawlers, including one or two that belonged to British United Trawlers, the firm owning the *Gaul*, carried Royal Navy technical officers to calibrate satellite navigation equipment − a duty supposedly performed for the Admiralty's Hydrographic Department.

Built by the Brooke Marine Company in 1972, and originally named *Ranger Castor*, the *Gaul* was a single-screw stern trawler whose first owner was the Ranger Fishing Company of North Shields. As a stern trawler, she was considerably in advance of the smaller and older side-winders, in that not only did her stern facilities allow a much greater catch to be brought over the sloping stern ramp, but this same catch could also be processed and frozen whilst still at sea. Known in Hull as 'the Hilton of the High Seas', vessels such as the *Gaul* also had much improved facilities for the crew. In each of the cabins there were carpets and fitted furniture, whilst a video recorder, television, film projector and laundry were also available. More important, perhaps, was that such mundane tasks as the gutting of fish no longer had to be undertaken on the unprotected upper decks, but upon the factory floor below.

Arriving in Hull during 1973, the year in which she had been purchased by British United Trawlers, and subsequently given her new name, the *Gaul* was quickly recognised as one of the safest trawlers ever to operate out of that port. In common with three sister ships, also purchased from the Ranger Fishing Company at this time, she had numerous built-in safety features that included a steel-strengthened hull for additional stability and de-icing equipment operated from the bridge. Furthermore, from the point of view of her sudden disappearance, before which no distress signals appear to have been sent, it should be noted that she had three separate radios, each of which could be operated upon an emergency battery should the main generator be damaged. The vessel also had additional buoyancy that was created by the large hollow factory deck which should have been sufficient to keep the vessel afloat for the sending of such distress signals. Finally, despite a crew of only thirty-six, she had sufficient liferafts for fifty, each of which was fitted with distress signals.

It was on 22 January 1974, at exactly 06.05GMT, that the *Gaul* sailed out of Hull, bound for the north coast of Norway. It was to be her third voyage for British United Trawlers, the company being more than pleased with her performance. She had already proved herself capable of handling the fierce Arctic weather, whilst her crew was amongst the most experienced in Hull. In the wheel-house that morning, still planning the actual course to be taken, was skipper Peter Nellist. As it happens, this was his first voyage in the *Gaul*, but Nellist was an experienced trawlerman, having been carefully instructed as to the handling characteristics of his new charge.

An hour or so after leaving Hull, the vessel hove-to off Bridlington, taking on board an extra hand. This was seen by some as the first of several strange incidents surrounding the loss of the *Gaul*. Who exactly was this final crew member? According to the owners, the man picked up was a certificated seaman needed for a vacancy in the crew list. Others have seen the arrival of this man as something far more sinister. An additional event, also somewhat unusual, was the belated discovery of a stowaway. After all, who would wish to make an unremunerated voyage to the fishing grounds of north Norway during the very depths of winter? According to the owners the man was drunk, and perhaps desperate for employment. Again, others have given this a more sinister interpretation.

On 26 January, the *Gaul*, having reached the coast of Norway, put in at Lodingen. This particular diversion was made necessary due to an injury sustained by the mate, George Petley, who had to be put ashore, being later flown home. On the 28th, continuing her voyage north, the *Gaul* put in at Tromso, where Maurice Spurgeon joined her as a replacement mate. Sailing at 2.30 that afternoon, the trawler then made direct for the Norwegian fishing grounds, conducting her first trawl on the 29th.

All, at first, seems to have gone well. The *Gaul* continued to send daily reports as to her position, whilst both her skipper, together with the new mate, were frequently to be heard communicating with other trawlers in the area. Spurgeon, in particular, would call up the *Swanella*, one of the sister ships to the *Gaul*, and exchange news with William Brayshaw, mate of that particular vessel and a lifelong friend. One such conversation was conducted on the morning of 8 February, the day of the *Gaul*'s disappearance. At the time both vessels were some 200 miles from the Soviet coastline with the weather becoming increasingly severe, winds estimated to be verging on gale force 8.

It was, in fact, fairly typical for the time of year, and certainly nothing that would worry a modern-day trawler. Easily within sight of one another, Brayshaw later reported the *Gaul* to be stationary and lying abeam of the weather. The *Swanella*'s mate also noted the soon-to-be-lost trawler to be well lit up, with her massive stern doors closed. All, therefore, was much as it should be. Towards the end of the conversation, much of it fairly trivial and relating to fishing prospects, Spurgeon happened to mention that they were about to dodge further into land — a tactic which would take her closer to Soviet territory.

On that day the *Gaul* was to make one further radio transmission, communicating with the *Orsino*, another of the Hull stern trawlers operating within the Artic circle. Transmitted at about 10.30am, it was one of several regular broadcasts in which the position of each trawler was given, together with an indication of any immediate problems. Such messages were then relayed directly to Hull. Any trawler failing to report was then presumed to be in trouble. As the position of the *Gaul* had been given the previous day (then given as 75° 15′N, 24° 50′E) and she had only moved slightly since that time, the *Gaul* was simply reported as having no problems.

The weather throughout that day continued to deteriorate. A force 8 gale gave way to a force 9, with winds gusting up to 10; the sea was churned into a raging mass of foam with mountainous waves, some 30 or 40ft in height, crashing into the *Gaul*. For anyone but a seasoned trawlerman it would have been a frightening experience. On board however, most doubtless took it in their stride. Certainly this particular stern trawler should not have had any difficulties. Force 9 gales were nothing new in the Arctic, and the *Gaul* was specifically built to survive such conditions. On board the *Swanella*, William Brayshaw was later to recall the severity of the storm, referring in particular to three huge waves that followed in quick succession. Everybody was thrown off their feet, whilst a 3in section of steel on the bridge was bent like a piece of tin.

It was at 4.30 during the same afternoon that the *Gaul* should next have transmitted her position to the *Orsino*. Even though no such broadcast was made, it did not at the time seem particularly unusual; a great many vessels reported in late, whilst the *D. B. Finn*, another Hull trawler, was not to check in for two days. Nevertheless, the *Gaul*'s failure to meet her transmission time was relayed to the trawler offices at Hull. On the following day, when the *Gaul* once again failed to meet her transmission time, cause for concern was finally realised. Unfortunately, for reasons that are not particularly clear, the information failed to be acted upon for a further day. On the morning of 10 February all British United trawlers were requested to search for the *Gaul*, whilst shortly after midday the Norwegian Rescue Co-ordination Centre at Bodo was placed on full alert.

Over the next few days a total area of 177,000 square miles was to be searched by trawlers, warships and aircraft – British trawlers operating in groups of six, each five miles apart. At the time a NATO exercise had just been concluded in the area, allowing the Royal Navy to dispatch the aircraft carrier *Hermes* and the frigate *Mohawk*, whilst the Norwegians involved the frigate *Stavanger* and the fishery protection vessel *Andenes*. Aircraft brought into the search included RAF Nimrods and Norwegian air force Neptunes, both of which carry highly sophisticated search and rescue equipment. Fierce gales and freezing temperatures severely hampered the search, with winds gusting between force 7 and 9. At times waves were said to be 25ft and 28ft high, with snow showers also reported. Despite, the extensive search, eventually concluded at 4.00pm on 15 February, not a trace of the missing trawler was discovered.

In Hull it was the small fishing community that surrounds the Fish Dock and Hessle Road that most grieved for the *Gaul*. Whilst not all crew members had links with this area, coming from towns throughout the North East, the majority clearly counted this as their home. A close-knit community with its own traditions, meeting places and language, it was from here that earliest demands were made for renewal of the search. Too many questions remained unanswered, whilst the lack of wreckage suggested that the trawler could not just have succumbed to the elements. The nation, as a whole, was in the midst of a general election campaign, and upon this the loss of the *Gaul* was quickly to intrude itself. Within the town of Hull, three marginal seats were up for grabs. As a result, three of the candidates pressed the then Prime Minister, Edward Heath, to honour the wishes of the Fish Dock electors and mount a second search. A man of the sea himself, he felt honour-bound to agree. For this reason there was a belated return to the Arctic Ocean by an RAF Nimrod. Mainly looking for wreckage, it concentrated for two days upon the waters surrounding Jan Meyen Island. Even though this particular Nimrod was joined by two Norwegian helicopters from Bodo, not a single piece of wreckage was to be found. The *Gaul* had truly disappeared without trace.

Rumours in Hull, some of which were of a most incredible variety, now began to be fanned. Most persistent was the suggestion that the missing trawler had been arrested and towed into a Soviet port. Entering the limelight at this stage was the wife of an exiled Russian nobleman, the Countess von Silvert. Recently returning from Denmark, she brought to the people of Hull the incredible story that a Danish radio station, *Dansk 2*, had actually announced that an English trawler, which they named as the *Gaul*, had been seen under close Russian escort. As for her own interest in the affair, the countess had a brother on the trawler. She admitted, however, that she spoke not a word of Danish, and that she only gathered this information from a few occasional words that she managed to recognise. To confirm her story, her husband, the count, went to the local police station where they, too, had apparently heard the news story. No record of this broadcast has since been found, but the countess is hardly surprised. She claims that the Danish Government has simply been told to keep quiet about the whole affair. Even today, though, some of the relatives of the missing crewmen believe they are held in a Russian prison camp. In December 1981 a Christmas card was addressed to the supposed survivors, being sent courtesy of the Soviet government. Needless to say it was returned with a curt note that disclaimed all knowledge of the *Gaul* or her crew.

How likely it is that crew members of the ill-fated vessel languish in a Soviet gaol is difficult to say. As William Brayshaw intimated during the subsequent enquiry, Soviet seamen would have had to have been 'supermen' to have boarded any vessel during the storm which blew up on 8 February. But as to the possibility of it being far fetched, this is certainly not the case. In 1927 the German trawler *Scharnhorst* and her crew were presumed lost; that is until the same trawler was discovered firmly encased in the Arctic ice near Cape Kanin in the White Sea. It later transpired that the crew, or at least those who survived, had been forcibly removed from the *Scharnhorst* and imprisoned within the Soviet Union. Whilst the Soviet government was reluctant to admit that they had imprisoned the crew they were, apparently, quite prepared to forward letters, addressed to them.

It was in May 1974, with wild rumours still circulating, that the first and only piece of *Gaul* wreckage was discovered. A lifebuoy with the legend *Gaul* clearly imprinted upon it, was found by Arnt Olsen, skipper of a Norwegian whaling vessel. Less than 200 miles from the last reported position of the *Gaul*, it was assumed that the buoy had floated up from the wreckage below. Arnt Olsen, for his part, expressed some surprise at the condition of the buoy, it being totally undamaged and in near pristine condition. Anyway, realising the importance of his find, Olsen took it to a local police station for later removal to London.

Once in the United Kingdom it was quickly established that this was a genuine lifebuoy from the *Gaul*, it even having the name *Ranger Castor* still visible in places. The rest, however, was not to prove quite so straightforward. A subsequent Admiralty examination proceeded to pose several new problems. According to their expert, the lifebuoy had never been submerged in water of a depth greater than 60ft. This, of course, effectively ruled out the possibility of its having been released from a trawler which, if lying at the bottom of the Arctic Ocean, would have been in water of 900ft in depth. Other tests also indicated that the lifebuoy carried only limited amounts of seawater plankton, with additional freshwater plankton. According to Arnt Olsen, the piece of wreckage had been found some 18 miles offshore, making it impossible for freshwater plankton to survive. Indeed, these Admiralty findings even suggest that the lifebuoy might deliberately have been planted in an effort to stem some of the wild speculation with which the residents of Hull were being besieged.

Many of the facts relating to the lifebuoy were brought to the attention of that official enquiry already briefly mentioned. It did not, however, take into account the full implications so presented. Instead, an attempt was made to explain the relative lack of plankton. It was, of course, rightly suggested that all plant plankton needs sunshine. Additionally, it was pointed out that in the Arctic Circle between February and April there is precious little daylight. But, as was later shown in a revealing television documentary screened some twelve months after the enquiry had completed its findings, the lifebuoy had been found on 8 May, a time of year when the sun shines for twenty-two hours in every day. This same programme, carefully researched by members of the Thames Television *This Week* team, also quoted from a restricted report that had been available at the time of the inquiry. Emanating from Norman Hendy, one of the world's leading experts on marine biology, it declared:

> Given the intensity of growth during April and May, it would be safe to say that the meagre growth on the belt could have developed in a matter of days.

The inquiry called to examine the loss of the *Gaul* sat through September and part of October 1974, meeting in the Victoria Galleries, Hull. Its eventual conclusions should have laid to rest all of the speculation that surrounded the trawler. In its final report it was clearly stated that the vessel had:

> . . . capsized and foundered due to taking a succession of very heavy seas on her trawl deck when she was almost broadside to the sea,

which initially caused her to heel over, and that she had not time to recover before a subsequent wave or waves overcame her ability to right herself. It seems likely that initially she was thrown so far over that those aboard her were unable to transmit a distress message.

In arriving at such a verdict Barry Sheen, QC, who headed the investigation for the Wreck Commissioners, took into account the weather conditions described by William Brayshaw and his acceptance that the vessel could well have been swamped if she had been caught by such waves whilst broaching the wind. Apparently, as the inquiry discovered, it was the habit of many skippers to indulge in the practice of turning and running into the wind solely for the purpose of maintaining position. Another influential witness was George Donaldson, chief naval architect of Brooke Marine, who also confirmed that should the *Gaul* have been broadside to the particular waves described, then she could well have lost stability. Certainly stern trawlers were more likely to take on water, with the volume of water not always being cleared by the special draining ports prior to the arrival of the next wave. As such, Donaldson indicated, his company had this in mind when, in the stability book issued to all skippers, they warned of water accumulating in the factory area. If, for instance, Donaldson stated, the *Gaul* had been running with the sea and then turned to head into it, during the act of turning she could have been 'lifted by the crest of the wave and fallen on her side', being then struck by waves, she would then have been pushed over.

At first, a published report produced by the inquiry did bring an end to the more extreme theories as to the loss of the *Gaul*. But it did not entirely destroy the notion held in some quarters that a top-level 'cover-up' was involved. Indeed, some of the bereaved publicly referred to the inquiry as being nothing less than a 'whitewash'. Much of their evidence had been discarded with an insensitive degree of bureaucratic formality. As to the feelings of at least one relative, these were demonstrated in October 1974, when Mrs O'Brien, mother of James O'Brien, spare hand, refused to have his name entered upon a memorial plaque to lost

177

crew members of the *Gaul*. She, for one, felt that her son was still very much alive.

A year later rumours had not completely died down. In fact they were to be given a sudden impetus by the discovery of new evidence uncovered by researchers working for *This Week*, the highly regarded news background programme that has previously been referred to. Apart from revelations relating to the lifebuoy, mostly gleaned from the official Admiralty report, they also produced evidence that British trawlers were being used as spyships. In 1971, for instance, it was revealed that the stern trawlers *Ross Illustrious* and *Lord Nelson*, both owned by British United Trawlers, had received, for a period of approximately six weeks, the very intercept receivers that the Royal Navy had previously denied were being used in trawlers. According to Stan Kent, a night watchman at the Fish Dock, he had seen naval officers instal equipment which he later identified as electronic devices that could only be used for monitoring military radio emissions. The television programme did go on to state, however, that no evidence existed as to similar equipment ever being placed on board the *Gaul*.

Alternative theories to explain the loss of this single Hull trawler quite naturally abound. One of these, and certainly the most credible, puts forward the view that she may well have been struck by a submarine engaged in shadowing the trawler.* It must be remembered that the *Gaul* was only 170 miles from the Soviet coastline, had a sophisticated collection of aerials for its own television and radio receivers, and might well have been thought a spyship. The result would have been the mandatory assignment of a vessel, in this case a submarine, for purposes of ensuring that the *Gaul* did not enter a sensitive military zone. Whilst the submarine probably had no intention of sinking the *Gaul*, the severe storm which could well have thrown the submarine to the surface, might well have resulted in a collision so severe that the trawler was holed. This and this alone, would explain why no radio signal was received. Having been holed, and twisted to one side she would have immediately lost her buoyancy and would then have sunk within seconds. Perhaps, also, ships of the Soviet navy may well have been involved in a clean-up operation to prevent the West from realising an incident had occurred. A slightly differing scenario, but leading to a similar conclusion, would be that of a collision with a NATO submarine. In this case the submarine, again thrown to the surface, might well have been shadowing the Soviet submarine already referred to.

It should at once, however, be stated that a collision with a submarine is not, by any means, the only plausible theory as to the demise of the *Gaul*. Equally she might well have been destroyed by one of the two contending cold-war powers. If she was a spyship, heading into land to avoid the storm, then a NATO warship might have been employed to prevent possible capture by the Soviet navy. Similarly, of course, the USSR may well have destroyed her as a warning. Either way, of one thing most people are certain, the *Gaul* sank sometime on 8 February 1974, but as to exactly how, this could be information privy only to a small naval élite.

---

*Trawlers and other ships have certainly been victims of submarines in the past. American submarines alone, during the decade 1965–75, were involved in at least nine collisions with Soviet vessels. Other NATO navies, usually less forthcoming, can also recount a number of similar incidents.

15

Disaster Ships

On the oceans of the world, even in this day and age, mystery still abounds. Increasingly though, many unexplained events surround but one type of vessel: the tanker. Laden with oil, chemicals and other noxious substances, a frightening number have ended their days in tragic and mysterious circumstances. Subjected to strange disappearances or violent and usually unexplained explosions, they are a type of ship which man finds difficult to control.

Perhaps the earliest tanker to create any sort of mystery was the *Ottawa*. Owned by the Anglo-American Oil Company, she left Norfolk, Virginia, on 2 February 1921, bound for Manchester. Four days later, having undertaken a routine exchange of radio messages with the British steamer *Dorrington Court*, she was completely to disappear.

The *Ottawa*, of course, was nothing like a modern-day tanker. With her engines aft and bridge amidships, she lacked the long, sweeping, uncluttered foredeck of the present-day 'super ships'. Launched in Newcastle during 1888, she was one of the earliest of her breed, registering 2,742 tons gross.

Another tanker that disappeared during those early years of oil conveyance was *La Crescenta*. Outward bound from Port San Luis, California, she was due to reach Yokohama, Japan, on 24 December 1934. The voyage across the Pacific should have taken no more than a month. Leaving Port San Luis during the last week of November, she was in radio contact with the *Athelviscount* on 11 December. At that time all was reported well. It was the last to be heard of her. In January, however, the *Athelbeach* reported passing through pools of oil at a point not far from the last given position of the missing ship.

It is likely that the true reason for the loss of both these tankers will never really be known. *La Crescenta*, a vessel with a poor reputation, was generally considered to be overloaded. On top of this, she was an ageing vessel, owned by a company who chose to spend little on her upkeep. One crew member declared in a letter home the vessel to be 'a proper old ramshackle'. This was a view also held by her captain, N. S. Upstill. In a letter to his wife, written during a previous voyage, he declared 'that the vessel was getting pretty old and that there was always trouble through breakdowns'.

More recently, there has been the disappearance of the *Grand Zenith* (31,000dwt*), a Panamanian-registered tanker that left Teesport in England on 19 December 1976. Bound for Providence, Rhode Island, she carried a full load of refined oil for use by the New England Power Company. Like the two earlier tankers she failed to reach her destination. On 30 December, whilst off the east coast of America, her captain, T. K. Tsou, reported that she was entering heavy weather. No further communications followed. A subsequent search, mounted on a fairly massive scale, revealed only two life jackets, both carrying the name of the ship.

Perhaps the mystery of the *Grand Zenith* carries some sort of parallel with the fate that befell another giant tanker some nine years earlier. In June 1968, the *World Glory* (46,434dwt), having entered heavy weather whilst off the Cape of Good Hope, simply broke in half. Nothing of this might have been known if the event had not been witnessed by other ships close at hand. According to Captain Obidth of the *Chevron Frankfurt*:

> We saw an unidentified ship pounding through the seas. Then there was a flash. We saw her break in two. Then came flames which lit up the clouds. We couldn't do anything.

As oil tankers go, the *World Glory* was an old ship, having

---

*Dwt: deadweight tonnage. Measurements of modern tankers is usually expressed in terms of their actual carrying capacity, otherwise known as the deadweight tonnage.

been built in 1954 by the Bethlehem Steel Corporation of Massachusetts. At that time she was one of the biggest ships of her class, able to carry nearly 50,000 tons of oil. The years, however, had aged her badly. Inside she was heavily corroded. Buffeting her way through the huge waves encountered off the Cape, the vessel could withstand no more. Her internal strengthening members gave way, and the ship started to break up. Worse followed. With oil pouring into the water, combined with the presence of highly inflammable gases, sparks from the splintering steel touched off an explosion that destroyed much that was left. Of a crew of thirty-six, only nine survived.

Tankers are particularly susceptible to structural failure. Partly this results from ownership by firms, many operating under so-called 'flags of convenience', which prefer to keep costs to an absolute minimum. Avoiding all but essential repairs, such firms frequently commission ships that are far from seaworthy. Another problem relates to the methods that are used in the construction of tankers. Most are prefabricated, a not altogether appropriate procedure when the tremendous strains of an ocean voyage are borne in mind. These vessels, with their excessively long hulls, are quite unable to ride huge waves, having to simply smash their way through. Considerable damage frequently results.

The tanker, therefore, because of potential failures in structural design, is an extremely hazardous vessel. This can be no better demonstrated than by reference to the single year of 1979. During those twelve months, no fewer than eighteen tankers were lost through explosions, the majority of which can never be explained with any degree of certainty. The most serious of all, resulting in the loss of fifty lives, occurred on 8 January. Early that morning, following discovery of a small fire, the *Betelgeuse* (115,000dwt), then lying moored in Bantry Bay, exploded like a giant bomb. Flames spread everywhere, creating a scene reminiscent of Dante's Inferno. For a time, also, it looked as if the fire might well engulf nearby storage tanks containing 1 million gallons of oil. Fortunately though, with the help of specially equipped tugs and numerous fire engines brought from the surrounding area, the inferno was brought under some sort of control. The *Betelgeuse* herself continued to burn for a good many hours, sending huge clouds of thick black smoke high into the sky.

The *Betelgeuse*, an ageing 'super tanker', was owned by the French oil firm of Total. Having left Ras Tanura in the Persian Gulf early in December, she was originally to have unloaded at Sines, south of Lisbon. Poor weather forced a rerouting to Leixoes, but it proved impossible to enter the harbour, a ship having sunk across the deep-water channel. Eventually, then, the *Betelgeuse* found herself destined for the Bantry Bay terminal which is situated at the western end of Whiddy Island.

Like a good many tankers which still trade upon the high seas, the *Betelgeuse* was a ship well past her prime. Already, a sister ship, *Casiopee*, had been condemned for scrap, with Total in the process of selling the *Betelgeuse* to an Arab shipping firm. Built in 1968, the *Betelgeuse* according to a survey undertaken in 1977, was 65 per cent corroded. This was far beyond acceptable limits, but despite their knowledge of this fact, the French oil firm neglected to inform the master, a failure which in the event almost certainly proved fatal. Unaware of her extensive weaknesses, the master of the *Betelgeuse* placed her under considerable strain during the passage to Ireland. In the Bay of Biscay, as a demonstration of obvious faults, she suffered an extensive oil leak that had to be promptly attended to.

Following the explosion, an inquiry commissioned by the Irish Government not only established the tanker to be in a very poor state of repair, but went on to list numerous faults that also existed within the Bantry Bay terminal. Tugs which should have been on hand to give assistance, were stationed twenty minutes away, and not even within sight of the loading jetty; lifecraft were but irregularly inspected and evacuation training was unknown. Even more catastrophic, however, was the absence of personnel from the control room. This resulted in the fire being discovered at a very late stage, with the high-pressure water pumps only being operated after an unnecessary time lapse.

As to the cause of the original fire, nothing can be certain. Structural failure was certainly considered a possibility. Weakened by her voyage through the Bay of Biscay, the *Betelgeuse* was in a highly precarious state. Oil, initially pumped from the midship tanks, so affected the vessel that she actually began to buckle. Incorrect ballasting further exacerbated the situation, with the heavier fore and aft sections beginning to sink. Eventually, it is supposed, with various metal components beginning to shear, a fatal spark ignited the ever-present hydrocarbon gases. According to the report, this probably occurred at about 12.30am, and could easily have been brought under control at this point. Instead, it was left unattended for 10 minutes or more, eventually spreading to the entire ship and adjacent oil jetty. The retreat of many crew members was cut off, several jumping into the waters of Bantry Bay, drowning before the arrival of any rescue craft.

The Bantry Bay disaster received considerable publicity. Occurring in western Europe and resulting in the loss of so many lives, this is hardly surprising. Many similar disasters, though, receive little or no media coverage. Indeed, a great number of those oil tankers destroyed in 1979 were virtually ignored by the world's press. An exploding oil tanker is no longer news – especially if it occurs in the Third World. Typical of this was the lack of publicity given to the *Ioannis Angelicoussis*, another of those oil tankers totally destroyed in that year.

The facts surrounding the *Ioannis Angelicoussis*, are fairly straightforward. Greek registered and owned by a small company whose offices were once in Piraeus (the firm no longer exists), this particular tanker was built by Lithgows of Port Glasgow. Like the *Betelgeuse*, she was eleven years old and suffering from corrosion. In mid-August, contracted to load crude oil, she arrived at the oil port of Malongo, in Angola's northern Cabinda province. On the evening of 16 August, whilst completing operations, an explosion occurred in the forward part of the vessel. A fire immediately broke out, with flames soon leaping skywards. As at

Bantry, it took some twenty or thirty minutes for rescue craft to arrive, with the nearest tug situated 8 miles away. Fortunately, however, most of the crew were recovered, losses being restricted to a pumpman, two deck crew and a terminal worker.

The fire on board the *Ioannis Angelicoussis* continued for several days. So that damage to the terminal might be avoided, she was towed to a point some 65 miles out to sea. Here she remained, caught in the African/Equatorial currents, helplessly drifting in a series of ever-widening circles. Standing by, ensuring that she endangered no other shipping, was the marine supply vessel *Spartan Service*. Eventually, with further tanks exploding, the *Ioannis Angelicoussis* sank on 4 September.

The reason for the *Ioannis Angelicoussis* explosion, once again, is more or less impossible to determine. Structural failure, crew members smoking, or even static electricity, could each have been responsible. As those at Bantry discovered, an oil tanker in port, loading or unloading, is at its most dangerous. Vapour and oil leaks are all too easily ignited, and once set off the evidence is completely destroyed.

For the *Ioannis Angelicoussis*, however, there is also another possible cause, this time much more sinister. A chance exists that her destruction was no accident. Instead, she may well have been victim of a terrorist attack. Evidence for this comes from the captain of the *Herculean Service*, one of the fire-fighting tugs which first approached the stricken tanker. Involved in the rescue of crew members, he reported a strange hole in the bow and close to the likely point of explosion. With ragged edges turned inwards, it could only have been caused by a device placed on the outside of the hull.

Sabotage is not as far fetched as it might at first seem. Angola, situated on the west coast of Africa, is a newly independent state, desperately trying to create a socialist economy. It is a nation, however, with a great many enemies. In the south there is to be found UNITA, an anti-government guerilla force whilst in the north, and at one time operating within the Cabinda province, was the Front for the Liberation of the Cabindan Enclave (FLEC).

Both groups (the latter no longer exists) were supported and financed by foreign governments – namely South Africa and Zaire. Frequently mounting attacks upon important centres of the Angolan economy, it is quite possible that one or other was responsible for the destruction of the *Ioannis Angelicoussis.* This would have taken the form of small explosives placed along the hull, and laid by a highly trained squad. That such things occur is amply demonstrated by recent events in which mercenaries, trained in South Africa, and acting in support of UNITA, were responsible for the part destruction of the main oil refinery in the Angolan capital of Luanda.

In the world of shipping, tankers have an extremely poor reputation. Not only are they considered dangerous, but with many of them registered under the Panamanian, Liberian or Honduran 'flags of convenience', the skills of their crews are also open to doubt. A hopefully untypical example occurred off the Cape during December 1977. This was when the *Venoil* (325,728dwt), outward bound from Iran, collided with her sister ship *Venpet* (325,645dwt), then on her way to collect oil from Iran. It was a day of extremely poor visibility but despite this both tankers continued to cruise at full economic speed. In effect, this meant that neither tanker would be in a position to stop in a distance of under 2 miles. Furthermore, the radar on board the *Venpet* was found to be incorrectly calibrated.

The collision led to both vessels being abandoned, with over 30,000 tons of oil pouring into the already heavily polluted seas around South Africa. Yet it was a situation that could so easily have been avoided. The resulting inquiry discovered that the officers on board both vessels lacked adequate bridge training which doubtless explains why neither vessel communicated with the other and why the *Venpet* even broke the basic 'right-turn rule'.

With such an appalling lack of seamanship, though restricted to a minority of tankers, it is small wonder that accidents occur. During the past decade there have been more than eight hundred serious tanker casualties resulting from explosions, collisions and groundings. It is to be hoped that improvements in this dismal safety record are soon to be brought about. Numerous organisations are currently reviewing the entire subject, with the prestigious International Chamber of Shipping publishing, in November 1981, the report of its own specially commissioned 'Tanker Accident Working Group'. Initially established to investigate, above all else, the increasing number of unexplained losses, the report makes a number of pertinent recommendations. Amongst them it includes the suggestion that key personnel should have both greater practical experience and increased training, whilst ships themselves should be more frequently inspected and carry improved safety equipment.

Greater tanker safety will also ease the situation that surrounds an even more serious problem: environmental pollution. Over the years millions of tons of both crude and refined oil have been leaked into the seemingly limitless oceans. Much of this has emanated from oil tankers. Restrictions have therefore been placed both upon the amounts of oil to be released and the area of such discharges. Additionally, recent years have seen improvements in tank-cleaning techniques, no longer requiring oily water having to be ejected into the sea. Despite all this, ever-increasing amounts of oil have entered the oceans because of the high number of tanker casualties. In 1980 alone, according to the estimates of the United Nation's International Maritime Organisation, 420,000 tons of oil entered the sea from this one cause.

In many respects oil pollution really constitutes the final mystery of the maritime world. Such huge quantities of oil, especially if both permitted and illegal discharges are included, may be causing hitherto unrecognised problems. Certainly there is a possibility that a thin and suffocating oily surface film is being created which, given a sufficient length of time, will destroy the ocean's natural plant-life, upon which all other sea creatures eventually depend. Marine biologists, uncertain as to the extent of any damage, merely indicate it to be an urgent problem that requires an immediate remedy. How much time before the ecological balance is finally tipped is an unknown factor. It is at least one mystery that the world could afford to be without.

Bibliography

PRIMARY SOURCES AND MANUSCRIPTS
In some cases, and in particular when researching the loss of the *Bulwark*, personal interviews with witnesses were undertaken. Amongst those interviewed, therefore, were Commander Drage, RN (retd), then a midshipman on board the *London*; Mr W. Wadlow, then employed at the Isle of Grain air station, and Mr Arthur Plewis, then a pupil at one of the local elementary schools. With regard to the loss of the *Samkey*, I was in brief correspondence with Mr R. A. Beattie. For the most part, however, extensive use was made of both contemporary newspapers and documentation held at the Public Record Office. Amongst the latter were Colonial Office papers for Barbados (USS *Cyclops*), various Admiralty papers (mainly those concerned with the loss of such ships as *Bulwark, Glatton, Natal, Princess Irene, Royal George, Vanguard* and *Victoria*, together with relevant logbooks) and Board of Trade marine correspondence.

PRINTED SOURCES
Newspapers
Barbados Standard (1918)
Chatham News (1914–18)
Engineering (2 August 1907)
Fiji Times and Herald (1955–6)
Graphic (1879)
Groninger Courant (1849)
Hampshire Chronicle (1782)
Hull Daily Mail (1974–83)
London Evening Standard (1936)

Lloyd's List (various)
New York Fatherland (1915)
New York Times (1915)
News of the World (1874)
Sphere (May 1915)
The Times (various)
Virginian Pilot (1918)
Wellington Evening Post (1955–6)

Books
Baarslag, K. *SOS* (London, 1937)
Barnaby, K. C. *Some Ship Disasters and their Causes* (1968)
Blyth, C. and Ridgeway, J. *A Fighting Chance* (London 1966)
Bywater, H. *Their Secret Purposes* (London 1932)
Croix, Robert de la. *Mysteries of the Sea* (London, 1956)
Fitzgerald, C. C. P. *The Life of Admiral Sir George Tryon, KGB* (London, 1897)

Gardiner, Leslie. *The British Admiralty* (Blackwood; 1968)
Garrett, R. *Great Sea Mysteries* (Severn House, 1978)
Gilbert, M. *Winston S. Churchill, 1914–16* (Heinemann, 1971)
Gould, C. *Mythical Monsters* (London, 1886)
Gould, R. T. *Oddities* (London, 1928)
Hampshire, A. Cecil. *They Called it Accident* (London, 1964)
Hardwick, M. and M. *The World's Greatest Sea Mysteries* (Odhams, 1968)
Heuvelmans, B. *In the Wake of the Sea Serpents* (London, 1968)
Hickey, Des and Smith, Gus, *Seven Days to Disaster* (Collins, 1981)
Hoehling, A. A. and M. *The Last Voyage of the Lusitania* (London, 1957)
Jenkins, G. *Scend of the Sea* (Collins, 1971)
Junco, Yves de, *Les Naufrages de la Minerve* (Paris, 1969)
Keen, Tom, and Haynes, Brian. *Spyship* (Allen Lane, 1980)
Kusche, Lawrence. *The Bermuda Triangle Mystery – Solved* (New English Library, 1975)
Larn, Richard. *Shipwrecks of Great Britain and Ireland* (David & Charles, 1981)
Lockhart, J. G. *The Mary Celeste and other Strange Mysteries of the Sea* (London, 1965)
Lockhart, J. G. *Mysteries of the Sea* (London, 1924)
McDonald, Kendall. *The Wreck Detectives* (Harrap, 1972)
McEwan, G. J. *Sea Serpents, Sailors and Sceptics* (RKP, 1978)
Maddocks, M. *The Great Liners* (Time-Life, 1979)
Masters, David. *When Ships Go Down* (London, 1936)
Maughan, Robin. *The Joyita Mystery* (London, 1962)
Miller, C. *Baffling Mysteries* (Pan, 1976)
Mostert, Noel. *Supership* (Macmillan, 1974)
O'Donnell, Elliott. *Strange Sea Mysteries* (London, 1926)
Ortzen, Len. *Stories of Famous Submarines* (Barker, 1973)
Rintelen, Capt von. *The Dark Invader* (London, 1933)
Rogers, S. *Derelicts of the Sea* (London, 1937)
Rule, Margaret. *The Mary Rose* (Conway Maritime Press, 1983)
Sacaze, Rear-Admiral. 'La Perte du Sous-marin *Minerve*', in *La Revue Maritime* (1969) p432f
Shaw, F. *Famous Shipwrecks* (London, 1930)
Simpson, C. *Lusitania* (Penguin, 1983)
Snow, E. R. *Unsolved Mysteries of the Sea* (London, 1964)
Wilkins, T. H. *Mysteries* (London, 1958)
Willis, Jerome. *The Last Adventurers* (London, 1937)
Winer, Richard. *The Devil's Jaw* (Bantam, 1974)
Winer, Richard. *The Devil's Triangle* (Bantam, 1974)

Index

The names of ships mentioned in the text appear under 'Ships' in the index. British warships are indicated by the initials 'HMS' followed by their launch dates. The initials 'HMAS' refer to auxiliary ships of the Royal Navy, whilst American and Dutch warships are shown by the use of 'USS' and 'KNM' respectively.

Adaman Sea, 9
Aden, 131; Gulf of, 32, 129–30
Anglo-American Oil Company, 180
Apia, 13, 14,15
Arctic Ocean, 169–79
Atlantic Ocean, 22, 33, 127, 128, 138, 149, 152, 156
Aynon, George, 49

Banshee estuary, 73
Bantry Bay, 182–4
Barclay, Curle and Co, 73, 78
Beirut, 61
Bengal, Bay of, 9, 26
Bermuda, 140; Triangle, 127–8
Biscay, Bay of, 148–9, 184
Blue Anchor Line, 70, 73–4, 75
Blyth, Chay, 37
Board of Trade, 139
Bodo, 173
Boston, 152
Bourke, RN, Capt The Hon M. A., 66
Brixham, 9
Bruges, 147–8

Cadboro, Victoria, 33–4
'Caddy', 33–4
Cajueira, Isle of, 165
Canadian Pacific Railway Co, 87
Cape Hermes, 73
Cape Town, 70, 74, 75
Channel, English, 22, 47, 132–4, 150
Chatham, 65–6, 91, 92, 94, 151
China, 129
Cherbourg, 133, 151
Chesapeake Bay, 128
Churchill, First Lord of the Admiralty W. S., 83, 100–1, 117–18
Clyde, River, 133
Cromarty Firth, 91–2
Crozet Islands, 75

Darling, Bill, 26
Dens, Capt Jean Magnus, 28
Deptford, 39

'Devil's Triangle', 127
Devonport, 84
Drake, Sir Francis, 39
Durban, 70, 73, 74, 75, 77

Eddystone lighthouse, 22
Egede, Hans, 29
Elswick, 59
Emden, 105

Fakaofu, 15
Falmouth, 20–1, 34
Faversham, 20
Fiji Islands, 14–20
Firth of Clyde, 34
Flags of convenience, 182, 186

Galle (Sri Lanka), 26
Gibraltar, 13, 44, 48
Gloucester Harbour, 30
Good Hope, Cape of, 181–2
Grain, Isle of, 81, 82, 85, 87
Gravesend, 137
Greenland, 29
Greenwich, 42

Haifa, 61, 155
Hamburg, 146
Hamoaze, 46, 84
Harrison Line, 106
Hartlepool, 70
Hawke, Admiral Edward (later First Baron) (1705–81), 46
Helensburgh, 34
'Hoodoo Sea', 127
Houwink, Capt Derk H., 23
Howe, Admiral Richard (later Earl) (1726–99), 45, 46
Hull, 169–70, 173–8

Ilberry, Capt J. E., 73, 76
Indian Ocean, 25, 73, 75, 79, 127
Ingram, James, 50–1
International Chamber of Shipping, 187
Inverness, 94

190

INDEX

Irish Channel, 10

Jibouti, 131

Kempenfelt, Admiral Richard (1718–82), 45–6, 51
'Kilindini Monster', 34
King George V Docks, London, 136

Le Havre, 132, 134
Liberty ships, 136, 138
Likoni, 34
Liverpool, 100, 105, 115–16, 167
Livingston, Brockhurst, 119, 120, 124

M'Quhae, RN, Capt Peter, 31
Malongo, 184
Malta, 59, 61, 65, 66
Manchester, 180
Markham, Admiral Sir Albert Hastings, 58, 61–3, 66–8
Marryat, RN, Capt. Frederick, 50
Marseilles, 129–31
Masters, David, 21–2
Maughan, Robin, 19–20
Mediterranean, 56–69, 129–31, 153, 155–6
Medway, River, 43, 81–9
Melbourne, 76
Messageries Maritimes, 129, 131
Miller, T. H., 14, 19–20
Ministry of Transport, 136, 137, 139
Mombasa, 34
'Morgawr', 34

Nantes, 153
Nervig, Conrad A., 121, 128
New York, 13, 23, 101, 103, 104, 111, 116
New Zealand Shipping Company, 137
Newcastle, 180
Newfoundland, 25, 26
Norfolk, Virginia, 128, 180
North Cape, 169
North Sea, 33

Oceaneering Ltd, 113
O'Donnell, E., 22–3
Old Head of Kinsale, 102, 110
Orient Line, 130

Pacific Ocean, 127, 180
Peerless, Roger, 14, 16
Pendennis Point, 34
Peninsular and Oriental Steam Navigational Company, 130
Penlee, 142
Plymouth, 38, 45, 46, 47, 48, 51
Port Said, 129
Portland, 81
Portsmouth, 41, 42, 46, 60, 65–6; Harbour, 40, 44, 48–55, 155

Quiberon Bay, Battle of, 46

Ranger Fishing Co, 169, 170
Rangoon, 26
Ridgeway, John, 37

Rio Harbour, Brazil, 121
Roosevelt, Theodore, 112
Ross, Admiral Sir John Lockhart, 47
Rozel Point, 20, 21

St Brieuc, 20
St John's, Newfoundland, 25
St Nazaire, 131, 132
Santiago de Cuba, 136
Sayer, Claude G., 76–8
Scapa Flow, 92–4
Schoofs, Commodore of L'Atlantique, 132
Schweiger, Kapitanleutnant Walther, 105–9, 113
Seven Years War, 46
Shanghai, 129
Sheerness, 81, 82, 86, 87, 98
Ship Island, 176–8
Ships:
  AL2 (US submarine), 149
  Achilles, HMS (1905), 91
  Affray, HMS (1945), 156
  Agamemnon, HMS (1906), 83
  Andenes, KNM, 173
  Angora, HMAS, 88
  Aquitania (liner), 103
  Athelbeach (British freighter), 180
  Athelviscount (British freighter), 180
  Bellerophon, HMS (1907), 93
  Betelgeuse (tanker), 182–4
  Brunswick, 165–8
  Bulwark, HMS (1899), 81–92, 97–9
  Camperdown, HMS (1885), 56–8, 60–8
  Candide (merchant steamer), 106
  Casiopee (tanker), 182
  Centurion (merchant steamer), 106
  Chevron Frankfurt (tanker), 181
  City of Baltimore, 32
  Clan MacIntyre (merchant steamer), 70–4
  Cyclops, USS, 119–28
  Cydonia (British merchantman), 141
  Daedalus, HMS (1826), 31
  Dakar (formerly HMS Totem), 155
  D.B. Finn (trawler), 173
  Dei Gratia (US brigantine), 13
  Dorrington Court (British steamer), 180
  Earl of Lathom (schooner), 106
  Ekaterina Goulandris (Greek freighter), 151
  El Caribe (freighter), 142, 145
  Formidable, HMS (1898), 81
  Forte, HMS (1893), 75
  Fuller (salvage steamer), 75
  Galu Ar Mor (trawler), 10
  Gaul (formerly Ranger Castle), 169–79
  Georges Philippar (French liner), 129–31, 132, 134
  Glatton, HMS (ex-Norwegian Bjoergvin), 95–7
  Golden Hind (formerly Pelican), 38–9
  Gorgon, HMS (ex-Norwegian Nidaros), 96
  Grand Zenith (tanker), 181
  Great Galley (Great Bark), 42–3
  Guelph (passenger steamer), 78
  Gulflight (tanker), 103
  Harmanna (Dutch galiot), 22–3
  Harry Escombe (tug), 75

Henry Grâce à Dieu, 40–1
Herculean Service (tug), 185
Hermes, HMS (1898), 75
Hermes, HMS (1945), 44, 173
Hopestar (freighter), 137–8, 140–2, 145
Iberian (British steamer), 33
Implacable, HMS (1899), 81
Invincible, HMS (1977), 44
Irresistible, HMS (1898), 81
Ioannis Angelicoussis (tanker), 172–4
Jena (French warship), 99
Joyita (launch), 13–20, 24
Juno, HMS (1895), 103, 106
Kaisar-I-Hind (liner), 130
La Crescenta (tanker), 180
La France (liner), 134
L'Atlantique (liner), 131–3, 134
Leicester (freighter), 139–40
Le Touareg, 151
Liberté (French warship), 99
Lion, HMS (1910), 94
London, HMS (1899), 83, 85
Lord Nelson (trawler), 166
Lusitania (liner), 10, 100–18, 134
M-1, HMS (1917), 150
Marine Sulphur Queen (tanker), 142
Majorca (coaster), 10
Mark (freighter), 10, 142, 145
Mary Celeste (brig), 10, 13, 15, 24
Mauretania (liner), 103, 134
Mikasa (Japanese battleship), 99
Minerve (French submarine), 153–5
Mizar (oceanographic research ship), 153
Myngs, HMS (1914), 95
Narrung (cargo liner), 78
Natal, HMS (1905), 91–2, 93, 94, 97
Neptune, HMS (1909), 93
Nuestra Senora de la Concepcion (Cacafuego), 39
Ondine (French submarine), 150–1
Orsino (trawler), 172
Otranto (merchant steamer), 130
Ottawa (tanker), 180
Ourang Medan, 9
Palatina (merchant steamer), 79
Pandora, HMS (1900), 75
Paul Lecat (liner), 131
Pearl (schooner), 25–8
Peel 12 (trawler), 110
Phoebus (merchant steamer), 86
Pittsburgh, USS, 120, 122, 127
Prince of Wales, HMS (1902), 83, 85
Princess Irene, HMAS, 87–8, 97
Queen Elizabeth, HMS (1913), 94
Ross Illustrious (trawler), 178
Royal George, HMS (1756), 44–55
Sabine (merchant steamer), 75–6
Samevron (merchant steamer), 139
Samkey (formerly Carl Thusgard), 136–7, 138, 139, 140, 145
Scharnhorst (trawler), 175
Scorpion, USS, 152, 153, 156
Skylark, USS, 152
Sovereign, 41–2
Sovetskaia (tanker), 130
Spartan Service (tug), 185

Sportsman, HMS (1942), 151
Stavanger, KNM, 173
Strathowen (merchant steamer), 26–8
Swanella (trawler), 171, 172
Sybylle (formerly HMS Sportsman), 151
Thunderer, HMS (1872), 60
Titanic (liner), 100
Trieste (bathyscaphe), 152
Tuvalu (steamer), 15
U-20, 105–9
U-109, 33
UB-65, 146–9
Umfuli (steamer), 32
Union Star, 145
Vanguard, HMS (1909), 91–5, 97
Venoil (tanker), 186
Venpet (tanker), 186
Veronica (barque), 157–68
Victoria, HMS (1887), 56–69
Victory, HMS (1765), 45, 46
Waikato (steamer), 75
Waratah (cargo liner), 70–80, 123
World Glory (tanker), 181–2
Zebrina (schooner), 20–2, 24
2326 (French submarine), 151

Skegness, 34
Smart, John, 51–2
Spithead, 47
Sri Lanka (Ceylon), 26
Suez Canal, 127–9
Sûreté Général, 129
Sutton Pool, 23
Suva, 15, 16
Swan Hunter, 137
Swansea, 21
Sydney, 74

Thames, River, 38–43, 137
Thimble Thicket, 25
Tilbury, 139
Tokelau Islands, 13, 14
Toulon, 99, 153, 154
Tripoli, 61, 62, 65
Tromso, 159
Trondheim, 29
Tryon, Admiral Sir George (1832–93), 56–9, 61–4, 66–9
Turner, William Thomas, 103, 104–5

Union Castle Line, 75, 78

Vanderbilt, Alfred G., 102
Vanua Levu, 15
von Forstner, George, 33
Vulcan, A. G., 146

Waghorn, RN, Captain Martin, 46, 48
Wallsend, 137
Whitstable Shipping Company, 20
Williams, G., 14, 16
Wilson, President Woodrow, 100, 112, 114
Wischoten, 23
Woolwich, 38–43, 46, 59
Worley, USN, Capt George Wichman, 119–28

Yokohama, 129, 168